the
THREE SUPREME
gifts

*A Practical Approach to Self-Mastery
and to Transforming Your Life
Here and Now*

LISA HROMADA

an imprint of Sunbury Press, Inc.
Mechanicsburg, PA USA

ARS METAPHYSICA

an imprint of Sunbury Press, Inc.
Mechanicsburg, PA USA

For information about special discounts for bulk purchases, please contact Sunbury Press Orders Dept. at (855) 338-8359 or orders@sunburypress.com.

To request one of our authors for speaking engagements or book signings, please contact Sunbury Press Publicity Dept. at publicity@sunburypress.com.

ISBN: 978-1-62006-201-2 (Hardcover)

Library of Congress Control Number: Application in Process

FIRST ARS METAPHYSICA EDITION: August 2019

Product of the United States of America
0 1 1 2 3 5 8 13 21 34 55

Set in Bookman Old Style
Designed by Crystal Devine
Flower vector created by freepik (www.freepik.com)
Cover and Illustrations by Lisa Hromada
Edited by Lawrence Knorr

Continue the Enlightenment!

"WHEN LOVE IS GIVEN,
when one does for the reason other than the self,
not expecting a return while understanding
that there is always a return,
one has reached wisdom.
That is a very significant statement
that concludes tonight's session."

—WISE ONE, THURSDAY, SEPTEMBER 9, 1982, SESSION 234
EXCERPT FROM
LOVE IS THE SEED: TEACHINGS FROM THE SPIRIT WORLD
WWW.LOVEISTHESEED.COM

DEDICATION

May this exploration of the *three supreme gifts*
help empower you to create the life
that you desire, with grace and ease.
May it give you all that you need
to find within you a renewed sense of self
and the ability to fulfill all that you came here to do
while fully enjoying the many blessings of this life.

�֍

Download free meditations, practices, prayers,
and other resources at
www.LoveIsTheSeed.com

CONTENTS

INTRODUCTION

The Three Supreme Gifts: A Practical Approach to Self-Mastery and to Transforming Your Life Here and Now ("The Three Supreme Gifts")—a companion book to *Love is the Seed: Teachings from the Spirit World*—is a practical, divinely guided approach to self-mastery and it is intended to be a guide, not for the purpose of perfection, but for the purpose of aligning yourself with the flow of life available to you right now. This flow is guided by a non-physical part of you in companionship with God and all other souls who share this human experience.

In my first book, *Love is the Seed: Teachings from the Spirit World*, I share a fascinating collection of conversations based on over 200 handwritten sessions with Spirit. You will find references to these sessions throughout this book. Within *Love is the*

Seed: Teachings from the Spirit World, I introduce nine core teachings from the spirit world. *The Three Supreme Gifts* is the first of those core teachings and is the very foundation by which that <u>spiritual</u> part of you and the <u>physical</u> part of you come into harmony.

The Three Supreme Gifts is only a small portion of what was shared during the sessions that occurred in the early 1980s. It was the Fall of 1981 when my father began to channel messages from guides, well-known leaders throughout history and other loving souls, while my mother took detailed dictation of every word that was spoken. Within the nightly sessions included in *Love is the Seed: Teachings from the Spirit World* are messages about love, consciousness, death, and the afterlife, reincarnation, God's laws and creation, and answers to questions you ask yourself when in search of your own enlightenment and sense of purpose.

Love is the Seed: Teachings from the Spirit World helps you better understand yourself as Soul, reveal what you must learn in this life and beyond this one life, and guide you to a greater awareness of your connection to all. If you yearn for answers and desire to reconnect with who you really are—a loving creation and extension of God—I invite you in *Love is the Seed: Teachings from the Spirit World* to "come sit with us" for the nightly sessions.

The Three Supreme Gifts, as a companion book, is intended to transform your life here and now, and help you to more consciously grow beyond negative karmic and thought patterns and living, which in turn not only changes the course of your life at the very moment you begin to apply these supreme gifts, but forevermore. The future then changes for the better where you can fully embrace and live in the blessings that are and have always been available to you. God forsakes <u>no one</u>. God is with you for whatever purpose of good that you desire to create.

If you have ever wanted to know the meaning or purpose of your life, how to master or navigate your life, and really any question you may have about your life, it all comes down to what you have at this very moment. What you have are *love, thought,* and *free will.* This is what you are gifted with, for your benefit and your empowerment to create a life of greater joy. It is truly incredible.

You are about to delve into a subject of love, thought and free will from a different perspective than you may have previously considered. The perspectives contained in this book have to do with aspects of your relationship to and connection with: (1) this divine guiding presence that is God, the One Consciousness of which you are a part and (2) your physical, conditioned experiences here on Earth as *personality.*

Although this detailed exploration of the three supreme gifts will certainly guide you to a deeper understanding of how each of these gifts provides you full empowerment over your life, my intention is to give you greater awareness to the depth, breadth, and nuances of each element of love, thought and free will. It is these gifts that directly benefit your life, on a practical, moment-to-moment, day-to-day basis, affecting every aspect of your life—body, mind, spirit, imagination, community, relationships, emotions, work and finances.

Along with this in-depth exploration of the three supreme gifts, my intention is to give you useful, practical, easy to implement practices that you can do anytime, no matter how busy your life is. Every day I come across people who are so involved in the "doing" in their life and "their story" in this life, that they have forgotten the gifts inherent within them and the purpose of their creation and for coming into this life.

I too have experienced getting lost in the "doing" of life. There is a level of unconsciousness at work where you get so caught up in thinking and doing that you miss the flow of your life. It happens for nearly everyone I meet. And when it happens, it causes suffering in one form or another—through feelings of guilt, anger, frustration, impatience, resentment and a "world-out-to-get-me" problem after problem mentality.

Your life is not meant to feel this way, yet it can be easy to find yourself stuck in a pattern that does not benefit you. After all, your life calls you in various directions from work to family to responsibilities as a neighbor and citizen. So, if you find yourself saying, "I don't have time to focus on making things better," or "it's going to be too much work or time," the useful, practical and easy to implement practices that I have provided in this book are especially for you.

In the following pages, I provide not only quick practices but also an explanation of your purpose as *soul*, your purpose as *personality* through which your soul has this human experience and I share details and an interpretation of each of the three supreme gifts that Spirit spoke so much about in *Love is the Seed: Teachings from the Spirit World.*

What it all comes down to is what you are given in this life for your highest benefit and liberty. You are given everything that you need to achieve higher and higher degrees of awareness, enlightenment, and understanding. Despite being somewhat accustomed to hearing about what my parents experienced and their communications with Spirit, I will forever be in awe at what was shared for the benefit of all having this human experience. And upon finding what resonates with you most in the following pages, relax in the knowing that through the three supreme gifts you can create a life of <u>much</u> greater joy, ease and inner peace at the level of your physical body, as well as your mind and spirit.

CHAPTER 1

YOUR DIRECT PATH TO DIVINE EMPOWERMENTS

To begin truly transforming your life and mastering your "self" to the absolute best of your ability, it is helpful to understand your connection to God—that divine guiding presence <u>within you</u>—and your connection, as soul, to your physical, conditioned existence as *personality* living out this human experience. Only then can you find greater meaning in the three supreme gifts. And only then can you get the most benefit from the recommended practices. These practices are dedicated to strengthening and enhancing your ability to get the most enjoyment from your life in new and genuinely incredible ways.

What I discovered as I pursued this path to understanding the three supreme gifts is that these gifts <u>alone</u> that you have access to right now, encompass

<u>all aspects</u> of this life in form—this conditioned existence—in a way that once they are understood, they can completely shift your life into the direct path in alignment with the light of love, grace, mercy and compassionate wisdom that is God.

And in doing so, you more fully live a blessed life with less stress and more fulfillment. Your role and responsibilities as mother, father, spouse, sibling, employee, business owner, neighbor, and so on don't cease; they become more divinely directed. And the way that you feel, view and respond to the world around you and your role becomes more holistically beneficial.

Despite this human experience being one of contrast, which translates as experiencing the unconsciousness and free will of others who do harm, injustices and cause stress or devastation, your perspective changes. And the divine energy within you shifts in a way where you no longer identify with and get continually sucked into the negative emotional effects of outside circumstances.

To put it simply, you shift your life from perceived problem after problem and stress after stress, to enjoying a flow of life where you feel liberated with clarity and a greater connection to the universal energy that is provided by that piece of God that is within you.

Honestly, when I started to take an in-depth look into why these three supreme gifts are so important to understand and why they are emphasized repeatedly in the book *Love is the Seed: Teachings from the Spirit World*, I was simultaneously brought to tears and illuminated with excitement, renewed wonder and awakened in many ways to the absolute gift of this life. Despite knowing on a surface level that life is a gift, I did not fully understand the empowerment bestowed upon us all, until I began to dissect the words of Spirit.

❈ *Your Link to the Blessed, Beneficial Life Meant for You*

I discovered an enlightening link between the three supreme gifts in a way that completely shifted how I looked at every aspect of my life and how, with simple steps, this physical, conditioned life can be instantly transformed. Such a shift eliminates the constant frustration and feelings of disconnect, naturally strengthens your spiritual connection and lights your path in new ways to the blessed, beneficial life you are meant to have.

With this shift within me came a pursuit to illustrate this link in an instantly attainable manner that I can share with you. It led me to create quick practices for each of the three supreme gifts that ultimately lead to self-mastery in a way that allows you to still be fully present for all your responsibilities—kids, family, work, etc. And the practices allow you to more fully enjoy and expand on your life's blessings and have greater clarity and peace in response to your life's heartache and challenges, all while strengthening your connection to your higher "Knower" Self and to God.

The practices introduced in this book are created in such a way that they don't take you away from your pursuit, ambition or drive of what you wish to accomplish; they are designed to elevate you to more clarity <u>as</u> you pursue your passions, because these practices eliminate much of the doubt and mind chatter that often takes you off course.

It is not important that you know every nuance to each of these three supreme gifts. What is important is that you take what resonates with you most first and work from there. Understanding, practicing and embodying even just one concept and putting into practice one element from each of these gifts puts you significantly closer to this blessed beneficial life that you desire.

What happens when you implement the practices introduced in this book is you consciously align yourself with the healing enlightened energy of divine love. What many are unaware of is the eternal, continuous presence of divine guidance. This loving divine guidance lives within you and expands infinitely out. In the book, *Love is the Seed: Teachings from the Spirit World*, Wise Ones often describe the qualities of God and reinforce the messages that God is a part of all—all are within God and God is within all. There is no separation, except perhaps the perceived separation that some believe themselves to have. While you may not see or feel this guiding presence often, because of what I call *the invisible veil of conditioned existence*—negative thoughts, emotions, and beliefs that you get caught up in—this presence exists, and you are a part of it.

Fortunately, you get glimpses of this presence often throughout your life, specifically when you are amid an inspired creation. Take for example a writer who is inspired by a new idea and sits to write. As he begins to write, the words begin to flow effortlessly and quickly, and born within them is a renewed breath giving life to whatever he is creating through his writing. In inspired moments such as these, you tap into this energy of divine guidance that is ever-present.

❀ UNDERSTANDING YOUR CONNECTION WITH GOD

❀ *The divine guiding presence that is within you.*

Imagine for a moment that you are standing where you are currently, and you are looking out in front of you. Within arms-reach of you, stands this pure white or gold light. It is like a ball of light and energy pulsating in a gentle rhythm. And then out of this ball of light, a form begins to reveal itself and you realize with an inner knowing, as the "knower soul" that you are, that standing in front of you is God, or Jesus,—or whomever or whatever resonates with you, and you recall in this very moment the true essence of who you are. This light, you can imagine is your divine guiding presence.

You innately know that this pulsating energy also lives within you. With outstretched arms and a silent, still and loving energy, you feel this light reach out and fill your entire body and being. Even if you can't feel this energy at this very moment, believe that it is right there with you, because it indeed is, and it accompanies you wherever you go.

If you choose, you can close your eyes now momentarily and imagine yourself reaching out your hand toward this ball of divine light. Visualize this light and energy flowing in through your hand and filling your entire body with healing, loving energy of clarity and wisdom. Imagine how as it flows and moves within your body, it is giving you more energy, clarity and cleansing any negativity or tension that you may be holding onto. You are being started anew and you have access to this divine light and energy at any time. It is the very seed from which your soul was created.

❋ The Heaven that Exists Within

As referenced in the book, *Love is the Seed: Teachings from the Spirit World*, the order of the three supreme gifts is love, thought and free will. These are the supreme truths that all souls come to understand. And in the words of the Wise Ones within the nightly sessions, you must live enough experiences in various divine schoolhouses, Earth being one of them, to come to this truth. When that understanding comes, you *know* it, you *feel* it and it is in what Spirit terms, "heaven."

Heaven exists anywhere where the truth of the three supreme gifts is lived, felt and understood. In a session documented in *Love is the Seed: Teachings from the Spirit World*, from Notebook #28, Page 4, a Wise One describes this heaven as "infinite grandeur, splendid understanding, indescribable happiness and peace" that is reality.

Within you lies your future, past, and present. In various sessions with Spirit, it becomes clear that you as a soul have had and will have many lives and experiences here on Earth to help guide and direct your path to wholeness or ultimate enlightenment; and that there are many ways for one to be "reborn." And while you will have lifetimes of experiences here on

Earth, you can be reborn the moment you make the conscious choice to make shifts in your life for the better and pursue a more wholly beneficial life, in faith and companionship with that part of God within you.

✤ *The Purpose of Your Soul Upon Creation*

When your soul was created, you were created out of that pure light of love—that omnipresent, omniscient energy that created All—so it would make sense that you, at your very core are a piece of this pure light of love, of God.

Upon your creation as soul, you innately knew that you were a part of this love, but what you did not yet have was <u>wisdom</u>. This is something that you, and each soul that comes into existence and into this life in form, seek to acquire—the compassionate wisdom and full understanding of what it means to "be love." And through this love is your path to wholeness or completeness.

Imagine the moment that God created your soul or any soul for that matter. I imagine this soul as an infant child who innately knows the feeling of "love," because there is nothing else in its reality that challenges that knowing, but what it does not yet have is the wisdom to fully understand love, which includes everything that God is—love, grace, mercy, compassionate wisdom, the giver of empowerments, and the full embodiment of *love-given*.

Love-given refers to the giving out of love without asking for or requiring anything in return. Through this energy of *love-given* God created your soul and all souls. It is love without condition and it is a <u>pure</u> love that benefits all souls.

Every decision about coming into this life and all experiences you set forth to have are made from the energy of *love-given*. This love is, in fact, what is at the seed and the very essence of what you are. In various sessions in the book, *Love is the Seed: Teachings from the Spirit World*, Spirit highlights the significance of *love-given* in relation to souls' purpose in evolution by saying, "The soul, after experiencing, learning and understanding 'love-given,' is at one with the Creative Force." In other words, the soul innately seeks to understand and embody the wisdom of God ("the Creative Force")—not just be aware of it but reach and be fully united with the divine unconditional love of God; this is your soul's destiny and objective to be a living dynamic of this limitless love.

Your soul innately seeks this wisdom. One way in which the soul learns is through coming into this Earth experience in physical form. As a new soul, you know that upon your creation and upon coming into human form, you are given love, thought and free will. These three supreme gifts allow your soul the empowerment to create anything it envisions or imagines for you as *personality* living out this human experience.

❀ UNDERSTANDING PERSONALITY FOR SELF-MASTERY

❀ *Soul as Personality in this Human Experience*

It was a Wednesday night, February 17, 1982, and the one hundred and eighteenth session my parents had with a group of souls, most referred to as Wise

Ones. "Wise Ones" are souls that have been around for eons and are highly enlightened. Some of these souls may still be learning the infinite depth of love's truth and the three supreme gifts defined in this book, yet they are each at a point in their evolution and their "journey to completeness" that they are able to share details of these gifts with you, and all who come upon these words.

Within the February 17, 1982 session, which was handwritten by my mother, as was every session, a Wise One came through and revealed something that I would have glanced over had I not been writing this book. An excerpt of the word-for-word dictation is as follows:

"This is a Wise, Wise, Wise One. I Am That I Am . . . When mankind, as individuals, begin to <u>express</u> that eternal love, begin to <u>understand</u> that all are created equal in God's eyes, begin to <u>realize</u> that the justice in your hearts you shall have, begin to <u>accept</u> each element and individual right of free will expression without judgment, where that free will expression does not infringe upon the rights of other individual elements free will expression, that each element of God has consciousness, then peace will exist."

(You can read the full session in *Love is the Seed: Teachings from the Spirit World,* Chapter One, Mankind and Love.)

This excerpt speaks directly to those qualities of divine love, which are acceptance, patience, compassion, grace, mercy, et al, and how when you are having this Earth experience—living through the *personality* part of you—embody the three supreme gifts, you can find the inner peace and healing that you seek for yourself and desire to share with others. When you "express that eternal love," "understand that all are created equally in the eyes of God," and "accept individual rights to free will without judgment or infringing upon another's" peace will exist on an individual level and collective, societal level. The *thought* aspect of the three supreme gifts—love, thought and free will—is interweaved throughout what this Wise One is saying here. When thought gets involved though, it often takes you off course and hinders you from attaining the peace that you seek for yourself and your world, yet thought is also a significantly beneficial tool with which you are gifted, and I speak more about this aspect of thought in the following pages.

❋ From the Spirit World to the Human World

Imagine for a moment, you are in this dream-like environment that is beautiful and filled with light. You are not the personality that you are in this life, but you are a being of light. *Imagine this.* Imagine yourself as "soul." In this environment, there is at least one other soul or light being with you. And this light being is working with you to decide how your current life and personality that is "you," is going to unfold and develop. The general circumstances of your life are being created—the family you are born into, the probable things you will pursue and the probable challenges you will be faced with. What you can understand from the sessions documented in *Love is the Seed: Teachings from the Spirit World* is that there is a consultation of sorts in the spirit world before your birth to decide the purposes, creations, and goals of your human life.

In this environment, you as "soul" are reviewing past reincarnation experiences, what you desire to learn, your purpose for entering again into human form—whether for resolving a debt (karma) or for the sole purpose of love and giving. Simultaneously during this consultation, you make loving agreements with other souls. These other souls may be those who share this life with you and who are willing to help you in this life to experience what you need to for learning and evolving and vice versa. You can think of these other souls as "mom," "dad," "brother," "sister," "friend," and even "enemy." Each has agreed to share this life experience with you to help you fulfill your soul's purpose. Whether you have "good" or "bad" experiences with these other souls is irrelevant because all experience is out of love.

In this dream-like environment before coming into the human body that you inhabit today, you were in a realm of "absolute" where you knew you are *love* and are free from restriction or limitation. In this environment, there is no stress, there is clarity and acceptance. Then you are born into this life and forget most of this and must see your way through this conditioned Earth experience, to remember who you really are and why you came here. In other words, before incarnating into this life, you, as soul, knew your purpose for coming here; you simply have forgotten. Fortunately, you never need to feel lost or alone. You are always connected to that which you are a part—this divine guiding presence to help guide and remind you.

❊ Your Purpose as "Personality"

There is always a purpose for entering and re-entering life after life in form—a soul purpose, a karma purpose and a loving and contributing purpose.

This "loving and contributing purpose" is where the personality's desire for purpose can come into play. As *personality*, you are in a constant state of seeking and living out your purpose. The challenge for the personality is that along with living out this life as the personality of "James," "Sarah," "Kabir," "Ana," "Li Na," or whatever name you go by, you have external stimuli influencing your every decision and you have your own thought and free will to take whatever direction of your choosing. Your direction may not always be in the direction that your soul intended.

You may go in various directions in your pursuit for purpose and still feel that you are missing the mark or feel that there is something more significant that you should be doing. I believe that it is rare for a soul to come into this life for one big purpose to fulfill. Have you ever asked yourself (or God), "what *is* my purpose?" You may find that there is a pulling inside of you toward something that you can only describe as, *more*.

At the seed of this "more" is the pursuit of love and indirectly, or subconsciously, to find that part of God that exists within you. This love of God that resides within you translates here to needing purpose. Your purpose manifests your drive, desires, ambition, and all that you envision for a more fulfilled human experience as soul animating the "you" part—your *personality*. Your *soul* will endeavor to find what the best method is for expressing and having an experience that has a purpose and find that love for creating. Through your *personality*, what you seek to create is something tangible, whether it be what you envision for your family/social life or for your work.

As described in one of the sessions in the book, *Love is the Seed: Teachings from the Spirit World*, "When the soul is first incarnating on Earth within the order of the personality, the soul brings with it, eternal wisdom and understands that the purpose for incarnating on Earth is to practice eternal truths and not just know, but understand these truths." And this is done through your various experiences and through what you pursue to create for your life and work; it is through *living out your life* <u>*purposefully*</u>.

❃ *Asking Yourself the Right Question*

You are in a constant state of living your purpose. Rather than asking, "what is the purpose for my life?" you can instead ask, "what is the purpose of <u>this</u> moment, right now?" *Personality* often thinks about the past or the future. What helps is to think of and accept wherever you are and ask yourself what you *really* want. It goes back to declaring what you are willing to live and be. You may not have an answer to, "what is the purpose for my life?" but you may have an answer to what you are willing to live and be and what you ultimately want in your life. For example, if you are unhappy within your job, you may have an answer to what you are willing to live and be. That answer might be you're willing to live in a way where you can fully enjoy whatever job allows you the ability to have more time with your family. And you are willing to be of service to others through your talents.

There is a point at which you should stop seeking your purpose and just start living purposefully. Doing whatever you are doing "on purpose," intentionally and mindfully. And allow the flow of life to come more naturally, in its right timing and to reveal whatever next opportunities to express yourself and *experience* who you really are at your core and that next thing that you can call your "purpose."

There may still be yearning for *more* or knowing that there is more that you are meant to do. There always will be because you are constantly evolving into your wholeness, *through* this life that allows you to <u>experience</u> who you really are.

For as much as the personality part of you will continue to pursue and strive, the soul part of you will always try to call you back to remember why you chose to come into this life—and remind you at the seed of this purpose is always love.

❋ *A Perspective on Earth Life as Personality*

You come into this life and are born into your physical body, you develop and express yourself through your personality, you take on various roles and responsibilities, and you pursue various paths to finding your passion, talents, and purpose. In your life, you take on the roles of producer, director, and actor. As "actor," you are friend, lover, spouse, mother, father, and neighbor, and each day living out a part of the purpose of your life within each of these roles. While there may not be one big purpose, there is always a purpose and most often several purposes.

At the age of thirty-nine and while in the process of writing this book, I came across a cassette tape dated September 12, 1982. It was an astrology reading that my parents had done on me. I was just two years old at the time. It was fascinating for me to hear the accuracy of the reading as the facilitator described various aspects of my personality and the possible paths I would take in my life.

I was especially fascinated when she said that part of my purpose would be "to bring truth and discipline of the mind to the world." Growing up I recall my mother telling me about how within the sessions with Spirit, she and my father were told that I would be a speaker for God—"a spokesperson for the Creator" to be specific. I always wondered how that would manifest and when, and what that really meant. I pursued various paths for many years unrelated to being "a spokesperson for the Creator."

Plus, that sounded so "big." I wondered how I could possibly be a speaker for . . . God. What did I know about God, really? I pursued and acquired degrees in design and certifications in coaching, marketing and mentoring, and although I had spiritual experiences throughout my life, subtly interweaved my spiritual background in my work, and maintained a strong faith in this divine Source, Universe, God— or whatever term I was referring to this Creator of All at various times in my life—I did not foresee how this would be a part of my purpose.

In my late 30s is when I realized what this meant, and I began writing the book *Love is the Seed: Teachings from the Spirit World* and *The Three Supreme Gifts*. There came a point where I just *knew* the timing was right and the way in which I would do it felt right. Life was gradually calling me toward this over the years. I imagine that you can think of a time where you have experienced this; you became inspired to do something, to be of benefit in some way, the timing felt right, and you just *knew* and felt empowered to act.

Often the most valuable lesson you can learn about this aspect of purpose is to relax. Throughout the years, I found myself focusing so much on seeking a "big" purpose, that I was ignoring what was right in front of me. What I did not often realize is that through my seeking, I was taking action, trying various paths of service and pursuing specific goals (sometimes succeeding, sometimes not), and fulfilling *many* purposes—as are you.

Relax in the knowing that while you may not feel completely fulfilled at this moment—whether regarding your work or relationships, you are being guided to seek more. And what you are doing right now is, indeed, purposeful and is setting you up for something even more amazing. It is setting you up to fulfill what your soul set out in this life to accomplish—that pursuit of love, however that manifests for you. The added benefit in your pursuit for *more* is that you can naturally create a life where you find greater improvement and more frequency in experiencing feelings of joy.

> *"And you will make mistakes, you will make mistakes,*
> *you will make mistakes. You are fallible.*
> *Meaning simply do not let your errors dishearten you.*
> *Have courage and faith."*
> —WISE ONE, SATURDAY, OCTOBER 23, 1982, SESSION 253,
> *LOVE IS THE SEED: TEACHINGS FROM THE SPIRIT WORLD*

❋ *Degrees of Understanding*

There are levels or degrees of understanding that come about through experience. You may ask yourself *how* you can embody these truths or supreme gifts. The answer is over time. Understanding, or degrees of understanding, can only come at the moment when you are ready. You can compare it to looking at a problem over and over a thousand times and then suddenly you have clarity of the solution. Nothing changed about the circumstance or problem, but your degree of understanding changed, and you could see the solution.

Complete understanding happens over many lifetimes. However, given that you are here now reading these words, I believe that you are already making incredible shifts just by simply putting into practice this aspect of love.

As an example, when I first read the words from Wise Ones and other loving souls that are documented in the book *Love is the Seed: Teachings from the Spirit World*, there was a lot that I did not fully grasp or understand, so I just allowed the words to find their place within me without putting too much extra thought into them. Then, as I read more and rested on some of the phrases over time that stood out the most, I began to see or get evidence of their truth. This is a divine guiding presence at work bringing clarity.

When I went back over the same words and sessions later, there was a new, clearer understanding. There were many times where I would have these, "OHHH, AHA" moments and I could feel almost literally, even down to a physical level the truth of the words finding a home within me. From what spirit expresses throughout the sessions, this feeling is God at work, making his "home" within you, and within all.

So, as you are reading these three supreme gifts first simply see what words *feel good* to you and resonate or ring true for you. As this happens, over time the actual embodiment of the words, truths, and love will manifest in new and deeper ways in your life and you will see divine shifts happening for your benefit. Enjoy the gift of this divine guiding presence within you.

As expressed in the very first session presented in chapter one of the book, *Love is the Seed: Teachings from the Spirit World*, "Within each and all does God dwell. God asks only that you ask for the voice of God to be heard. Ask and the voice of God will begin from within, you will hear and dream messages . . . God is in you. The answer is in you. The only part of you found in others and that which binds you to others is *love*."

CHAPTER 2

THE
THREE SUPREME GIFTS
PRACTICE

Included at the beginning of each chapter of the three supreme gifts is a mantra to practice that is quick and simple. These mantras are empowering methods to significantly improve your quality of life, streamline the path to fulfilling your purpose and be the most service to yourself and others.

What led me to create these specific mantras stemmed from the understanding that most people live in a paradigm of conditioned, habitual problem-centered and ambition-centered living. It can be difficult to realize this problem-centered habit because it has a way of sneaking up on you, but it is the source of most, if not all your suffering and feelings of unhappiness or resentment in this life. It is an energy field that you can easily get lost in.

And ambition-centered living is also tricky because it can disguise itself as "purpose." So, in your effort to make a difference, find your purpose, do what you feel you are "meant to do," you lose sight of why you began the journey into this life in the first place. Additionally, when you are deep in the ambition-centered living dynamic, you naturally feed into the problem-centered energy field.

As an example, I know many amazing, giving and kind people—many of them parents—who, in their pursuit to fulfill a specific purpose or their vision of success, they cram as much as they can in a day until they finally are too tired to stay awake or they get themselves run-down. Upon waking the next day, their busy schedule starts all over. Between work, kids, spouse or partner, and additional passion projects or goals they wish to fulfill, they feel that there is no time to focus on improving their situation or they don't believe that they can.

Many years ago, I found myself busy all the time, trying to pursue a set of goals while working full time, taking care of my home and doing my best to make time for those I care about, yet I was completely unbalanced. I would complain that things were not flowing or coming easy for me and I found myself focusing on all the problems that needed to be resolved, but not actually the solution. When someone would point out that maybe I needed to take a break and that they were concerned that I was doing too much, I would say, "I don't have time to slow down."

Yet, I was also feeling like what I was doing was not coming easy, which in turn was taking more time and energy that I could have been productively applying to my goals. It was a miserable cycle. I was not nurturing any other aspect of my life—relationships, health, and so on, because of this focus on "making things happen." Little did I know at the time that I did not have to work so hard. Understanding the three supreme gifts has helped tremendously to reassess my goals and understand how to go about them with more ease and clarity.

The number one way I have found to elevate myself and others out of this problem-centered and ambition-centered living dynamic is with simple phrases that, when repeated, gently guide and ease the mind out of the vicious cycle of problem-focused living. Simultaneously, they help to redirect the ambition-centered living into a clearer, smoother path to a life of greater joy and the full empowerment allowing you to fulfill the purposes and work that you desire.

When my father channeled those sessions with Spirit that my mother dictated in the early 1980s and what is documented in *Love is the Seed: Teachings from the Spirit World*, Spirit could not emphasize enough the importance of understanding the truth encompassed within the three supreme gifts. In fact, the number one purpose for Spirit coming through was to share with you, and us all here living this Earth experience, the gifts each are forged with upon coming into this life.

They repeatedly emphasized how thought works in creating your reality, what the true meaning of love is and they offer a perspective on how you are intended to live your life through this energy of love and how you can use your free will in companionship with God to fulfill your purposes and enjoy the actual life journey here on Earth without all the stress that you feel on a regular basis. Essentially, they wanted to tell you that you can come closer to fulfilling the purpose that your soul set out to do without constant stress.

For example, in the Monday, November 9, 1981 session in Chapter Nine, Death and Reincarnation in *Love is the Seed: Teachings from the Spirit World*, a soul named Mike Rice spoke of life "over there," and emphasized, "Life here is not unlike certain situations on Earth other than there is not the stress here, for the most part. There is a greater understanding that love is truth and that life is infinite." What this means is that, both here on Earth and in the afterlife, the soul learns and has the empowerment to create anything it wishes for the sake of learning. In the afterlife, however, there is little to no stress, like you experience on Earth as the *personality* that is "you." Yet in both realms, here on Earth and in the realm of spirit, you can learn and fulfill a set of purposes, and you can choose to do so through experiencing stress or you can choose a more loving way.

For each of the mantras, you can choose to say them out loud or within yourself. When done throughout the day in split-second thoughts and actions, what you end up doing is <u>embodying</u>, living and being a purer, more authentic version of "you" that you were created to be. Soon you will see how this directly has a positive impact on the flow of your life. Through the mantras, you begin to find a greater connection to a divine field of solutions that is, indeed, available to you and within reach at this very moment. It takes just a small, conscious shift in focus, and my intention is for these mantras to help you get there more quickly.

SUPREME GIFT ONE

LOVE

"Love is the greatest truth, the supreme order of all."

—Wise One, Chapter 2,
Consciousness and Shared Reality,
Love is the Seed: Teachings from the Spirit World

CHAPTER 3

LOVE

"COMPASSION, GRACE, MERCY, PATIENCE."

"Compassion . . . grace . . . mercy . . . patience" is a remarkably empowering mantra and one of many that one may use for the supreme gift of *love*. The words chosen for this particular mantra bring together the defining essence of God and the divine essence within you, with healing energy that comes from the expression or inspired actions you put forth in your daily life. In saying this re-centering mantra, you are able to focus on the most important aspects of love and cut out the mind chatter that is often led by the ego.

When the ego is involved it often causes more problems because it looks for the solution from a one-sided perspective—through thought only. Problems are not resolved through thought. This mantra is a reminder of the qualities of divine love that you seek to embody. When you do, you allow that aspect of your Higher Self to take over and you can resolve conflicts and heal from heartache more quickly.

When you take action from this perspective of divine love, it is not about being selfless. If you don't first nurture yourself, you can't possibly be of full benefit to another. Just as when you are in flight and you are instructed, in case of an emergency, to put the oxygen mask on yourself before putting one on another. To be of benefit to another, you must first be in a healthy position yourself. It is about embodying these qualities as the foundation from which you act. It is about making decisions that honor both you and others involved, thus being wholly beneficial.

In the book, *Love is the Seed: Teachings from the Spirit World,* Spirit often refers to how "a love given is a love received" and that this is a just solution for life. You are always given what you give out. There is divine justice in this idea. So, when you make choices from the foundation and embodiment of the qualities of divine love, you can, both accumulate good karma by being of service to others in a wholly beneficial way and you can rise above aspects of karmic living into more direct connection with divine wisdom, clarity, and empowerments.

❋ *What It Means to Have the Love of God Within You*
You are born into this life and from day one, you are pure love. It is what you know and all you know. Engage with your son or daughter as an infant and aside from requiring necessities like food, care, and

safety, they seek out *love*—hugs, snuggles, a shared laugh or smile.

When your child is a toddler, you notice how they see the world through the eyes of love. They are amazed by every element of creation; they explore it, feel it with all their senses, admire it, appreciate it for the pure details of its creation. They love it in their own way.

And then throughout life, you seek love in various ways. Why? Because love is a reminder of who we are and what we were created to be. You are a part of the light of pure divinity. And this light is the radiant, omnipotent light of love. This love is the foundation that functions and guides your life here and now, and beyond this Earth experience.

Understanding even a fraction of what this divine love is and how it directly benefits your life can completely shift your perspective and all that you grew up believing. It can translate into renewed hope, acceptance of self and others, forgiveness, a positive outlook, commitment, a clearer sense of values, restored harmony and so on.

So then, what is love, really?

There is no one answer, but a place to begin is by understanding how love is defined on a spiritual level according to the Laws of God, which is referenced in the book *Love is the Seed: Teachings from the Spirit World,* and what it looks like in this human experience. In relation to God, the light of love, which is the love that is compassion, grace, mercy, and patience. This divine light of love is the giver of empowerments.

When you take this perspective on love into your life as *personality*, you can see it at work in many ways and you can *feel* the effects nearly immediately. You feel this when you are patient with another, express your gratitude for another, make a kind gesture, give a gentle touch on the shoulder when someone needs comfort and you can feel the effects of this perspective of love when you are demonstrating these qualities toward someone who your personality might view as unworthy of compassion, grace, mercy, and your patience.

As an example, let's say that a friend betrays your trust or says something to you in a way that deeply damages your relationship. A natural reaction from *personality* is to punish that person in one way or another. You may even want to "teach that person a lesson." Your personality may say, "How dare you? You are a terrible human being for what you did (or said). You don't deserve being a part of my life. You don't deserve good things." And your soul—with a greater understanding of the three supreme gifts—may say, "I see that you don't know the true damage of your actions. I forgive you. I will do my best to help you, while I nurture my-*self*."

In this example, it is an inner struggle between the personality's perspective and your soul's perspective, but you decide to follow your soul's perspective, as difficult as it is because your mind wants to hold onto the "wrongness" of their action. You begin by showing simple kindness toward this person whenever you see them and then gradually move into showing compassion and mercy. And in doing so, you will see the dynamic of your relationship change. It may be near immediate change if this friend is aware enough of the effects of their actions or it may be over time; it may be that they realize something within themselves that they want to change and it strengthens your relationship, or they may deny that any change needs to be made and your relationship may dissolve—temporarily or permanently. If it dissolves, then you find ways of re-centering your life using the exact qualities of compassion, grace, mercy, and patience, but this time toward yourself.

Love is both simple and complex to understand. And while it may not be possible to live every moment completely centered in this energy of love, you can consciously try to bring more of this energy into everything that you do and every interaction that you have. It is incredibly healing and what Spirit emphasizes within the many sessions that my mother dictated decades ago.

These qualities of divine love that you were created to embody are the exact ones that the mantra for the gift of love encompasses—compassion, grace, mercy, and patience.

When you "embody" compassion, grace, mercy, and patience, you embrace and give "form" to it. You personify this *love*. You mature as soul into this wisdom of the supreme truth of love and all that love includes.

Compassion from the human perspective is to recognize the suffering of others, feel deep empathy for another, desire to alleviate their suffering and take action to help. It is this divine love that can make you feel compassion toward another. You can say that this compassion stems from "shoes you once walked in." What this means is that you look at another who is less fortunate or experiencing some form of suffering and see yourself in them. You look at this other person and can imagine the possibility that you too, perhaps in a previous lifetime, experienced much of the same misfortune—that this was once part of the journey of your soul in this Earth experience. Figuratively speaking, this other person is you—the "shoes you once walked in." With this comes a new, heightened level of understanding of the common element that binds all humankind in this evolutionary journey of the soul.

Grace can be defined as divine light and energy that is always in motion to benefit all in creation. It is recognizing that everything is connected and to be cherished. Grace comes from the Latin word *gratia*, meaning thanks, favor, kindness or esteem. Various traditions around the world each have a similar understanding of the word "grace." Depending on the tradition, it can be defined as the unmerited favor of God, of infinite love and goodwill that God has bestowed upon humankind; the salvation of sinners and the granting of blessings; spiritual power; loving-kindness.

If *mercy* were to be described in one word, it would be "forgiveness." Many say that forgiveness is healing, and it is, yet it is also one of the most challenging to fully embrace. Without forgiveness, what you hold onto is resentment, guilt, unworthiness and other forms of emotional pain. When you hold onto the negative emotions, your entire being suffers— your body, mind, and spirit. You find yourself in an emotional prison, recounting the injustice done upon you until you can embody the elements of mercy.

Being merciful and healing is a process that requires you to forgive little bits at a time. You may even find yourself showing mercy on someone many times before being able to let go of the negative emotions holding you back from the peace that you seek. Mercy, in any case, does not mean you condone another's behavior, but that you understand the divine energy behind mercy, which is why I believe it is an important aspect to the manta under the supreme gift of love. With every effort of mercy is an act toward healing your-*self*.

Patience is an acceptance of the present moment, of another, of the timing of circumstances and of your own life plan. Patience is connected to love, understanding, acceptance, and faith. It is having faith in the working of the divine. In *Love is the Seed: Teachings from the Spirit World*, a Wise One describes patience as love, giving and receiving of love, living and believing in love, understanding and accepting that all things in the evolution of the soul are an infinite existence of God. When you run short on patience, negative emotions arise that in no way serve you. It is an opportunity though, a gift, to empower you to regain patience—to bring you back to that love, understanding, and acceptance to which Spirit calls you back.

When you act from this perspective of compassion, grace, mercy, and patience, you embody one leading quality of God—you become *a giver of empowerments*. Because when you live more from this definition of love, you emanate and illuminate this empowerment, giving others the authority or power that allows them to create what they desire for their life in a beneficial way. Imagine what your life and your world would be like when you impact another in this way. They then can have a positive impact on another and so on.

You can relate this to how plants pollinate. Just as "pollinators"—animals, insects, or the wind transfer pollen from plant to plant giving life and renewal to other plants—you, at the seed of your creation are love and you interact with the world around you and, whether consciously or by unintended consequence, you share this love, and all that this love is defined as, and give renewed life to another. Given that you are connected to all of creation, it is not a far reach to compare this aspect of the *giver of empowerments* to this natural, divinely created aspect of nature, renewal, and growth. This is what is possible when you embody this aspect of love; you become what you were created to be and come that much closer to understanding and embodying divine wisdom.

No matter where you currently are and what is happening in your life, it is my belief that you are closer than you think to this connection to divine wisdom through this gift of love. In chapter four on thought in *Love is the Seed: Teachings from the Spirit World*, it was Session 83, Sunday, January 3, 1982, that Spirit references how one is not limited in their ability to understand and embody this divine wisdom, that is unless they believe that they are. Spirit said, "For the wisest words on Earth and the wisest words in total consciousness, and the wisest thought on Earth and the wisest thoughts in total consciousness can be spoken by *anyone*. And they are always thoughts of selfless love. Of love-given."

❋ *Alternate Practices*

In addition to the mantra, "compassion, grace, mercy, patience," which can be extremely centering and beneficial, I want to share two more practices that may feel more relevant to you in certain situations. When you find yourself in situations where you need to find a solution or make a decision, I want to introduce this question to ask yourself; you can ask, "Given that I am a part of God and have within me compassion, grace, mercy, and patience, what is the best way to respond in this situation?"

Asking this question in this way allows you to first fully accept the divine within you, which for many, is difficult to do because we are often caught up in self-limiting beliefs. Second, it allows you to see the situation from a holistic perspective and one that is wholly beneficial—for both you and anyone else involved. In this way, you are intentionally living from the energy of love-given, which as we know from the many sessions with Spirit, is a fundamental Law of God who from this same energy created you—that which you give out is always returned to you. A love given is a love received. Answers, by asking yourself a question in this way, are most often revealed through inspired thought, a dream, a sign during the day, or another method to which you become awakened and aware.

One final simple straightforward practice is one that encourages you to allow and invite God to guide you. Think of any situation that you are in that you either have no control over, are struggling with, or that you have lost your inspiration or flow. Perhaps it is a relationship struggle, career struggle, creative block, or whatever it is that you no longer have the answers to or the energy to think about any longer. Then surrender whatever the struggle is to God.

You can say something like, "God, my friend, I have to make an important decision about (name the situation) and I don't know what to do. I am tired of feeling (depressed, frustrated, angry, unworthy, stressed, et al), so I'm now relaxing and surrendering this situation to you. I am open and accepting of answers to be clearly revealed to me with grace and ease. Please give me the clarity I need to make the right choice. I want to feel (worthy, happy, at peace, important, et al) and I need your help. Thank you."

You can even declare to God what action you are going to take, have taken and will continue to take in the situation—what you are willing to do, live and be—and then believe that God will take the remaining actions for your benefit. As an example, if it is a suffering work relationship where you feel undervalued by your boss or coworkers, you can declare that you are willing to do your best work and to be of service to others and then ask for clarity and help to resolve those things that are not in your control. Then relax and go about your daily responsibilities and notice any subtle differences that begin to happen for the better; they will indeed begin to be revealed. Each time you notice something for the better, say a simple thank you. God—this divine guiding presence—is indeed available to you for whatever good you may desire.

From the perspective of Spirit, love is about understanding what it means to have the love of God within you, what love translates to be in your life and then *embodying* those qualities. When you *embody* these qualities, you are, in essence, naturally connecting to your Higher Self and aligning with the energy of your Knower Soul—your soul that is aware and awake to "who you really are," beyond of your life in form. This is where you can find your connection to that divine guiding presence that is within you. In doing so, you can make the shift from a life of perceived limitations to one of true empowerment. You consciously make a declaration within yourself, and to that part of God within you, of what you are "willing to live and be."

�֍ *The Truth of Love*

During the last phase of my maternal grandfather's illness, his wife said she walked by and he was sitting up in the hospital bed they had for him in their small living room. She said he looked like a young boy, and she asked, "Pete, are you alright?" And he said, with a smile, as he stared off into the distance, "What a glorious day this has been." Then he laid back down. My mother recalls him telling her that he saw a male in a white robe who he felt was Jesus.

Years after his passing, in a session on August 24, 1981, my mother asked a Wise One about the vision that my grandfather witnessed the day he said those words. The Wise One replied, "He was allowed to see truth and all that is truth is God and all is God."

There are countless similar experiences expressed throughout the book *Love is the Seed: Teachings from the Spirit World* that speak to the truth of love. A truth that goes beyond words. Edgar Cayce, an American clairvoyant who spoke many times in the nightly sessions said, "I write of love and am still not able to describe the truth of love, for no words can fully express the truth of love, but the word 'love' itself. For love is the supreme thought by which all are created." In a Friday, November 27, 1982 session, my fraternal grandmother's husband came through and said, "I wish to say that there is only life and to say that love is greater than I knew." If you were to describe love, you might say love is just, mercy, beauty recognized, appreciation, giving, patience, genuine, eternal, purposeful, et al. In whatever way you describe it, the one common element of the whole aspect of love is that it is <u>truth</u>.

PRACTICES FOR SUPREME GIFT ONE: LOVE

MANTRA:
"Compassion, grace, mercy, patience."

QUESTION:
"Given that I am a part of God and have within me compassion, grace, mercy, and patience, what is the best way to respond in this situation?"

DECLARATION AND REQUEST FOR HELP:
"God, my friend, I have to make an important decision about (BLANK) and I don't know what to do. I am tired of feeling (NAME FEELINGS), so I'm now relaxing and surrendering this situation to you. I am open and accepting of answers to be clearly revealed to me with grace and ease. Please give me the clarity I need to make the right choice and feel (NAME HOW YOU WANT TO FEEL). Thank you."

SUPREME GIFT TWO

THOUGHT

*"In understanding that thought creates all,
a major step in creating is reached."*

—Notebook #17, Page 5,
Love is the Seed: Teachings from the Spirit World

CHAPTER 4

THOUGHT

"THERE IS <u>ALWAYS</u> A SOLUTION."

"There is always a solution" is one of the most empowering declarations and the ideal mantra for the supreme gift of *thought*. This affirming mantra brings tremendous harmony to any situation. When your thoughts are in harmony, this benefits every aspect of your human experience; it affects your physical body, your relationships with others and your feelings of joy, and it keeps your connection open to all the benefits that accompany the first supreme gift of *love*. In saying this mantra, you are able to instantly ease stress and clear a path to the answers and resolutions you desire, so that you can live the most satisfying and fulfilling life as possible.

There are two definitive aspects of thought: (1) your mental and analytical mind that can empower you to attain the greatness you came here to do, and (2) it is an energy field all its own and one that is fear-based, worry-based and problem-centered, and one that hinders you from achieving your goals and fulfilling the purpose your soul set out to do upon entering this life.

Thought is both *powerful* and *empowering*. Thought is *powerful* because it survives and thrives on the basis in your belief that your thoughts are your reality. What your thoughts tell you about yourself, a person, situation or an event, make it what it is. It guides your reactions to such things as well as your beliefs and future actions. These thoughts can hold truths, or they can be false depending on your perception of your thoughts.

Thought is *empowering* because through thought, ideas are sparked, and you are able to use thoughts to analyze and create whatever you choose to focus on. As you create, your thoughts at some point take a back seat and a natural intuitive flow takes over and you can create wondrous things. In other words, the empowerment of thought can guide you to more intentional creations and more effective use of the third supreme gift of *free will*.

In the book, *Love is the Seed: Teachings from the Spirit World*, one of the larger chapters is on thought. Part of the reason for this is because out of the three supreme gifts, *thought* is where you get the most stuck in this human experience. What we know from the sessions in *Love is the Seed: Teachings from the Spirit World* is that it is "thought" that creates. This means that you have the full creative power over your life, allowing you to essentially create any reality that you wish for yourself.

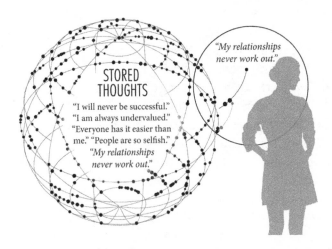

Because thoughts are energy, you can say that they have a life of their own. A thought is born, lived, experienced and when no longer needed, it ceases to exist in its original form. Thought alone is a state of confusion. Take for instance when a thought pops up in your mind that seems to come out of nowhere. Where does this thought come from? These types of thoughts often arise from like-thoughts stored within your subconscious from the past—whether a past experience in this current life or in a previous lifetime. Imagine for a moment that there is an energy field linked to you that holds your stored thoughts. I picture this energy field as a ball of tiny thoughts randomly circulating around within this energy field and every once in a while, a stored thought pops out and makes itself known within your mind. In its pure form, it has no benefit; it is just mind-clutter.

These thoughts are fleeting, but enough of the same thoughts that cause the same types of emotions—be it anger, resentment, jealousy, greed, et al.—is what is carried beyond this lifetime. So, in essence, a thought may be fleeting but it can live forever. According to the Wise Ones who spoke within the sessions in *Love is the Seed: Teachings from the Spirit World* thought lives in the memory of the soul.

When a thought is *felt* and internalized, causing a specific emotional reaction, the thought can live on forever until the thought is released. This internalized thought is held in the memory of your soul, lives on within the free will personality and carried lifetime after lifetime until you experience and learn enough through the specific thought-energy to let it go. And while you may not be aware of your experiences within past lifetimes, you can get an idea of possible stored thoughts by taking an in-depth look at recurring experiences in your life now, and how you *feel* on a regular basis. When the energy of the emotion sparked by the thought is no longer held, you can move on to better emotions, feelings, energy, thoughts, and ultimately a better, more enjoyable life. You move beyond the energy of that thought and it no longer is needed to be a part of your "reality."

Upon learning this and beginning to understand the true power of this energy of thought, which did not happen until my thirties, I began to pay closer attention to the thoughts that I was thinking and how these thoughts were making me feel. When I did this, I recalled back to my years as a teenager, and even back to my elementary school days, where I realized that deep down, I felt deeply insecure in many ways. There was a consistent pattern of this feeling that my thoughts were reinforcing, where I believed that I needed to prove myself.

I desired perfection in various areas in my life, from being the perfect friend, the perfect student, and the perfect daughter. Part of the reason for this desire for perfection was that I felt easily embarrassed making mistakes, which reinforced this feeling of insecurity. I worked hard to earn straight A's; I volunteered my time to contribute to charities; I strived for scholarships and I presented myself in a way that made my life look as picture-perfect as possible. If someone did not like me for one reason or another, it deeply bothered me, and I would strive for their approval. While the actions that I took were positive, kind and generous in many ways and came from an authentic place, I believe that there was a small part of me that desired to do those things so that I could feel confident, when deep inside, I did not.

The interesting thing is that there was nothing that I can recall throughout my life that would explain this feeling of insecurity. I knew my parents loved and supported me, I had close friends, friendly neighbors and I had good relationships with my teachers who, for the most part, were quite supportive of my success. To this day, I still have thoughts pop up in my mind of mistakes I made as a kid and how embarrassed I felt making mistakes. While I don't react to these memories in the same way as I used to, where I relive the thoughts and the *feeling* of embarrassment and insecurity, they nonetheless remain stored away and occasionally come up.

The emotion of "insecurity" comes just above the emotions of fear, depression and the feelings of being a "victim," which at times I also felt, especially off and on throughout my pre-teen and teenage years.

To begin finding my way through and out of this thought-energy of insecurity required that I first understand the truth of divine love and connect to that truth. The first major event that gave me the opportunity to experience this was when I took an impromptu trip to Paris, France one summer just a few months after my twentieth birthday. I was not intending to spend the summer there, but a series of events led me there.

It was like God said to me, "Ok Lisa, so you feel insecure? Let me show you the beauty that you are truly capable of." This "beauty" that you, I, and each are capable of is led by the three supreme gifts of love, thought, and free will. While I was not aware at that time of these gifts—those were not revealed to me in such a clear way until my late thirties—the truth and reality of them manifested in various ways to show me what I personally needed at the time to get beyond the thoughts and feelings of insecurity. And these gifts will manifest in your life in their own unique ways based on your own circumstances and the thoughts and emotions you wish to learn from and move beyond, that are causing you suffering.

While in Paris I became an observer of life. I could take myself outside of my own story and daily routine. While there, I did not feel like I had to prove anything to anyone. I rarely had contact with those back in the U.S. except for the occasional call, hand-written letter or e-mail. It was a time in my life where I had the chance to just be with my*self*. And I found that when you disconnect from most everything that you are accustomed to—even if just momentarily like when you go out into nature or hike, or when you paint, work on your car, et al.—you can expect to discover and get in touch with, who you really are. In Paris, I reconnected to the feelings of hopefulness, wonder, enthusiasm, passion, joy, and appreciation—this time toward myself. Being there allowed me to refocus and define a new set of beliefs without feeling the pressure that I allowed myself to feel back home.

There were many encounters and adventures in Paris that allowed me to see and experience each of the three supreme gifts with greater awareness, but there is one time that is particularly significant. Just up the street from the apartment in which I was staying, was the Cimetière du Père Lachaise (Père Lachaise Cemetery). The Père Lachaise Cemetery is the largest cemetery in Paris. It was one of my first landmarks that I visited and was one that I would frequently find myself. That first morning I was in Paris, I packed a snack and walked up to the cemetery. I recall a particularly still moment as I sat in the cemetery alone, amidst the quiet and I just observed my surroundings. All around me were huge headstones and family tombs that filled the cemetery and I felt, what I can only describe as, "being in good company." I was with my-*self*, with my thoughts and with this still silence of those memorialized there. I stopped thinking for a moment as I looked around and just listened to the silence. My thoughts then stopped, and I felt an indescribable joy.

I was feeling a connection that I had not felt in that way before; it was a feeling of love and somehow, I was connected to this love. It was a feeling of connection to all the creation that surrounded me. Given that everything that has been created comes out of this still, silent omnipotent divine presence, I innately knew that what was being created in that redefining moment was a renewed connection to that divine part of me that is within you, and everyone having this human experience. I began to see my-*self* differently. Where thoughts of doubt, unworthiness, and insecurity had once been, were being healed by compassion, grace and mercy, at first toward me and then toward others. I became more aware of this existence beyond "thought," and what is beyond thought is truth; and at the seed of this truth is love.

I came back to the U.S. from Paris with greater confidence in myself and a better understanding of what I wanted from my life and how I wanted to feel. Perhaps the most valuable lesson I learned from this trip, and that I want to especially share with you, is that it is not necessary to leave your life behind and travel to a far-off place to move beyond negative thoughts and their corresponding emotions and feelings to recapture the joy of your life. You can do it anytime, anywhere and starting now. Upon coming back home, I simply focused on being with people and doing things that made me *feel* good. And for those times that I was required to be around people or situations that previously brought up feelings of insecurity, I simply focused on many of the aspects explained in the supreme gift of *love*, and the "reality" of every experience shifted for the better, because my perspective and thoughts about them had changed. Once bound by fear, self-doubt, insecurity, darkness, or whatever negative thought and emotion you are feeling, you can now find yourself bold in faith—in yourself and in your connection to your

Greater Self. *Love* changes everything because with love comes acceptance, compassion, grace, mercy, and patience. Recall that love is not an emotion, but a state of being. And it is thought that can either help keep you in this state of being or pull you farther from it.

For further definition, it is thought that affects your emotions and what helps to build your belief system. The thought-energy is interpreted through the *feeling* of emotion and emotions, too, carry their own energy. You have a "thought-body" or what some call the "mental body" that carries energy, and you have an "emotional-body," or what some refer to as the "feeling-body" that carries an energy of its own, yet the two work together, either in harmony or disharmony. So, when you think enough of the same or similar thoughts and similar *feeling* thoughts, you essentially define your "reality." Yet, this reality that you have defined for yourself can lead to living out your experiences through an unhealthy *false self*.

When I speak of the "false self," I am referring to the layers of conditioned experiences that protect the personality. There is a <u>healthy</u> false self and an <u>unhealthy</u> false self. A healthy false self allows you to function and adapt to various situations and environments. Through this healthy false self, you utilize thought to assimilate and behave in a way that demonstrates such actions as politeness, friendliness, generosity or civility, even when you may not feel like it. A healthy false self essentially masks how you *really* feel for the sake of functioning in society while protecting your *self* from pure vulnerability in front of others, which can leave you open to negative or critical people. A healthy false self functions for the <u>benefit</u> of your <u>true self</u>.

Conversely when I speak of an <u>unhealthy</u> false self, I am referring to the thoughts and beliefs pertaining to your personality that create a reality that is detrimental not only to your desire to live an authentic life with greater joy, but it is these thoughts and beliefs that change your behavior, which come from a fear-based, or worry-based, perspective. Examples of this can be thoughts like, "If I am thinner, I will attract the right partner," or, "The more money I make, the more successful I will be." These types of thoughts led by the unhealthy false self, create a reality that is devoid of joy and causes an imbalance from the inside out. The intention behind these thoughts is not based on love for self or others, but on the worry of what others think or on thoughts that you will be a failure. An unhealthy false self functions to <u>benefit</u> an <u>unhealthy</u> false self <u>without regard for</u> your true self.

❋ How Thought Relates to Love and Free Will

What is one of the most interesting aspects about thought and why it is a gift and so important to harness and understand is that it sits right in the middle of love and free will, affecting both, either in a positive or negative way.

Thought can block the empowerment of love, which of course is that ultimate guiding system for your life and at the seed of your creation. And thought can negatively influence your free will. Thought, which typically works from the perspective of fear or worry, guides your free will actions, and these thoughts can easily be misguided, thus misguiding the actions that you take in your life.

❈ *The Byproduct of Thought*

There is an important and undeniable link between thought and emotion. A byproduct of *thought* is *emotions*, and emotions translate into *feelings*. Feelings are mental associations and responses to emotions and are highly influenced by your experiences from lifetime to lifetime—those built up beliefs, memories, and experiences. When you feel, it is like your body is producing an image and mentally assigning meaning to your emotion and determining your perceived reality. This is powerful and if not recognized, can steer you off course, distracting you from fulfilling the magnificence you came to do in this life.

These feelings drive more of the same thoughts, which leads to reinforcing or justifying your feelings. This often feeds negative energy that lives on in your soul. As mentioned previously, thought alone is a state of confusion. It is only when emotion is applied to thought and the emotion is felt, that *thought* is no longer just a state of confusion, it is whatever emotion and feeling you apply to your thought.

In other words, the process of thoughts, emotions, and feelings are cyclical in nature. You *feel* your thoughts through your emotions. Your emotions and how you gauge how your life is going, then spark like-thoughts, which reinforce your emotions and feelings, bringing more of the same. How do you know if you are stuck in a negative thought-cycle? You can simply ask yourself, "Do I feel good or not?"

If the reaction to the thought is that of good feelings, like bliss, love, and joy then you conclude that your reality is a good one. If the reaction to the thought is bad feelings, such as greed, anger, resentment, sadness or depression, you conclude that your reality is a bad one. Given that thoughts and emotions are cyclical—thought is reacted to and interpreted through emotion and the emotion causes you to feel a certain way that then causes you to have the same feeling thoughts—this aspect of "thought creates your reality" that Spirit spoke so much about in the book *Love is the Seed: Teachings from the Spirit World* becomes clearer. It also makes greater sense why Spirit emphasized "the empowerment to create anything you wish" through thought. You are empowered to make the choice to create a reality that either feels good or feels bad.

The thought, and the feeling(s) associated with the thought cease to exist once you interrupt the cycle of negative like-thoughts. It is challenging to shift from one type of thought-energy to a better one. In fact, it can be a constant battle. You can feel great one minute and then "bam," a thought comes in that reminds you why you felt angry, sad, defeated or whatever negative emotion you felt. And with this thought and feeling you respond in a way that does not feel good—you say something to someone that you wish you did not, isolate yourself from others, or maybe you replay the event repeatedly that triggered the thoughts within your mind, bringing about more negative thoughts. With a mantra like, "there is always a solution," you can consistently shift from one type of thought-energy to a better one. Like when exercising any muscle, the more you work it, the stronger it gets and the easier it becomes to see and feel results.

I will share a quick story about a woman that I have known since my late teens as an example. Since the day I met her, it was obvious that she enjoys life. She eats well and exercises, and to this day loves to socialize and has many friends. You would not know it from her upbeat attitude that she experienced the physical, mental and emotional effects of a stage three cancer diagnosis. Between the shock of the diagnosis, the treatments that took her hair, and the thoughts that her life that she enjoyed so much was in jeopardy of ending too soon, she had to make a choice: live in fear and anger or accept the diagnosis and make the absolute best of the situation and continue to be of service to others in any way she could. This required her to make a courageous shift from fear-based thoughts to better feeling thoughts daily.

She was determined to, no matter what, keep a positive attitude. She did this by choosing to do whatever that was in her control, to get through the treatment, keep living the life she loved and help others along the way. She went to work every day, took her treatments on a Friday so that she would be sick over the weekend, so not to miss work; she sang to others getting their treatments and brought food and flowers for the nurses every time she visited the hospital.

Despite having her down days, she continued to shift her negative thoughts into something positive. When her hair began to fall out, she bought a wig. One wig led to more wigs—all colors and lengths—and a whole new look and sense of self that the cancer experience and the negative thoughts associated with that experience could easily take away.

As referenced in sessions in *Love is the Seed: Teachings from the Spirit World*, thought seeks like thoughts. Any thought will live on as long as it can find and connect with like thoughts. Positive loving thoughts grow and are reciprocated, and conversely, negative thoughts attract negative thoughts, and thus negative energy. Given that thoughts take on a life of their own and "live" within you, even beyond this current lifetime, if you carry a negative thought vibration and never release it or resolve it, once you leave this life, the energy of that thought remains within you and will be carried to the next experiences of learning.

The sooner you can harness the power of your thoughts in a way that they become of complete service to you, the better, and more empowered you will be. This is what this woman could do when she was diagnosed with cancer. She used the empowerment of thought as a tool to continue living her life with purpose, joy, and love.

❋ Solutions Are Not Found in Thought

While thought can be an empowering tool when it serves to <u>benefit</u> you, with thought also comes worry. And there comes a buildup of fears and earthly pursuits that trap you in thought. When you are trapped in thought, you often look for answers outside of yourself—from mankind and from what mankind has created, as opposed to what *creative thought* has created. "What creative thought has created" means looking within yourself for answers and for that inspiration to create what you desire. It is within that you find your connection to love, clarity, the giver of empowerments and everything that God is and that part of you that is infinitely connected to the divine.

Where the energy and clarity of *love* get lost is in thoughts. You have external influences shaping your thoughts and enough of the same thoughts form your beliefs. Attached to those thoughts and beliefs are emotions. You <u>feel</u> these emotions, and they ultimately make up what you view as your "story" in this life. It is a cycle of thought after thought to solve a problem or analyze a situation, yet solutions, or answers, are never found in *thought*.

> *"Thoughts are tied with fear and when you get stuck in your thoughts, there is no advancement or improvement in happiness; there is just a build-up of fear and it feeds off itself and others of the same vibration."*
>
> —LISA HROMADA,
> LOVE IS THE SEED: TEACHINGS FROM THE SPIRIT WORLD

Just as your stored thoughts and memories influence the emotions that you feel and influence what you believe your reality to be, it works in reverse as well. You can suddenly feel something that is subconsciously linked to an emotion, which causes you to begin thinking thoughts that connect to memories and imagery that support that emotion. While emotions in their pure form are momentary, the feelings they conjure up and the energy behind those feelings can persist.

For example, you can be going about your daily routine and see a stranger who immediately triggers a feeling of anger within you. This feeling of anger has nothing to do with the stranger, but this feeling recalls thoughts of past events that originally caused the anger—perhaps of someone who betrayed you. This emotion of anger is momentary in and of itself, but within your mind, you begin reliving this memory and feelings of anger and may even take the thoughts farther and imagine other things that this person may have done to betray you. Your imaginative thoughts then go to what you should have said and what you now wish to say to this person. This thought-energy of anger is now taking on a life of its own and will continue to persist until you interrupt this cycle of negative thoughts. You can do this by going back to the mantra, "there is always a solution," or you can repeat a mantra that is just as divinely empowering, "I am releasing these thoughts with grace and ease." "Grace" and "ease" both reside in the energy of solutions—a divinely guided energy that is always available to you and that I speak more about in the following pages.

Because of this cyclical nature of thoughts, emotions, and feelings, without even being aware of why, your life can become an endless cycle of pain, confusion and other negative emotions. Think better feeling thoughts and you can make an empowering shift in your life. It often does not come easy, yet when you make efforts toward this endeavor, it has manifold rewards. The journey of your soul in this human experience is constantly encouraging you to grasp onto the unknown with faith and discard what no longer serves you—including thoughts—and that journey can be a sloppy one.

> *"Fear binds—love frees. Fear controls—love expresses.*
> *Fear holds—love gives. Fear is love seeking.*
> *Love is fear resolved."*
> —Friday, February 19, 1982, Session 119,
> *Love is the Seed: Teachings from the Spirit World*

❀ *The Original Purpose of Emotions*

Upon entering this life, you come into this human, physical body. Along with your physical body, you have your emotional/feeling "body" or guidance system, your mental/thought "body" and the empowerment of imagination that you can tap into to create a life you undoubtedly love living.

If you take into consideration that eons ago emotions alone originally helped mankind to survive by allowing for quick physical responses and reactions to environmental stimuli, you can understand the nature of emotions and ask yourself an important question when you begin to feel a negative emotion: "What is the perceived threat here?" If it is a physical threat, you act; if it is a mental threat, you know where to begin if you want to shift the feeling from fear and worry to empowerment, freedom, and love.

Conversely, your emotions and feelings are an incredible guidance system in this life and one in which you significantly benefit from. Your emotions allow you to experience your thoughts as "real." If you had no feelings, nothing would seem real. It is also your main tool for conversing between the physical "you" as personality and the non-physical "you" as soul.

When you can harness the *power* of your thoughts and learn to utilize the *empowerment* of your thoughts, you can live a more beneficial and joyful life through the *energy of solutions*, which is connected to divine love.

When it comes to love, and *feeling* "love," it does in fact have a physiological response and a mental response in that it brings thoughts that make you "feel good," yet *love* in the purest sense is not an emotion or feeling, it is a state of being and is all that you are created to be.

The reason why you don't see this love most times in others, or perhaps even in yourself, is because of the other factors that influence your thoughts, beliefs, and attitudes—who you believe yourself to be based on your upbringing, environment, and genetic makeup—which is all based in *thought*.

❃ *A Method to Deal with Your Thoughts*

I invite you to think of a situation now that you are currently experiencing that is causing you unease, grief, frustration or unhappiness. In this circumstance, ask yourself what you are believing about those thoughts and how those thoughts are making you feel. You can then ask yourself, "how is this feeling serving me in this moment?" While a bad feeling thought does not serve you well in living out a fulfilling, purposeful life that you seek to experience, the thought is serving a purpose in the way that it is letting you know that change is required.

So, *feel* the grief if that is what comes, *feel* the frustration, or whatever emotions you are feeling, then as soon as you accept the feeling and understand the reason behind the feeling, you can start the process of determining possible solutions and acting where you can, to <u>live out</u> that solution, <u>through</u> the gift of *free will*.

You will still inevitably be faced with strong negative emotions—feel frustrated in certain situations for example—but with greater understanding of your emotions, and thoughts behind the emotions, you can attain a heightened level of awareness where you more easily connect to your Higher Self and put the *energy of solutions* at work to find a solution. Additionally, an understanding that "I am feeling frustrated" and why you can move beyond the feeling faster and on to the next step of embracing the solution.

✳ Soul's Perspective on Attitude and Imagination
Along with this emotional setpoint—that emotional energy carried within your soul—you are born into this life with a specific attitude or disposition toward life and varying perspectives on the same stimuli. Your attitude depends partly on your genetic make-up, personality, and your desire and ability to imagine or visualize the reality that is most beneficial to you and that you most want. In a variety of sessions with Spirit, Wise Ones speak about the importance that attitude plays within this aspect of love, thought and free will. "Attitude" is defined as the degree of understanding, acceptance, and perception. One with a positive attitude gives off positive energy. One

with a negative attitude consumes energy. Through love, thought, free will and attitude, you as *personality* and you as *soul* achieve your destiny. In Session 29 in the book *Love is the Seed: Teachings from the Spirit World*, it was the personality of Albert Einstein that said, "This is why attitude in physical life is so important. A positive attitude helps you direct your life in concert with your soul, or essence, objective."

You likely know someone, or perhaps you are that someone, who naturally has a positive, almost laid-back and chipper outlook on life. You can experience the exact same stressful situation as another, but your perspective on and reaction to the situation is completely different. You are able to visualize and react to the situation in a different way.

Further understanding a great truth of the nature of visualization and imagination, what you may know but may not yet understand is that you have visualized your whole life and do indeed visualize your experiences on Earth. From the perspective of Spirit, when you understand this, you can dream great dreams. And when you dream great dreams, you can, if you choose, make them a reality. So, your attitude that you hold as you visualize and imagine, can mean the difference between creating a series of life experiences that you enjoy or that you desire to be different.

As a part of this human existence, in addition to having a physical, mental and emotional body, you also have an imaginative body. Through this imaginative body, you can visualize or imagine anything that you wish. And when you focus enough on this image of what you desire—be it a loving relationship, professional success, et al—I believe that given your connection to what Spirit terms as the "One Creator," of God—who visualized you and the entire universe into existence and gave you the same gifts to create anything you can imagine for yourself—that this endeavor toward attaining what you have imagined, can come into existence. What is most important is that you stay devoted to who you are and have faith that you can, indeed, create all that you wish to experience, live and be.

❈ *The Energy of Solutions*

There is <u>always</u> a solution. This solution is co-created with your higher consciousness—your Higher Self—which is in touch with the divine guiding presence within you.

When thoughts come up that cause you pain or suffering in some way, by repeating out loud or within yourself, "there is always a solution," your attitude and perspective about your life and your situation transform from a problem-centered energy zone to a solutions-centered energy zone. Here in this human experience, many, if not most, talk about one problem after another and because emotions are tied up in the energy of problems, it leads to physical problems, emotional problems, mental problems, and problems in your ability to imagine and manifest the life that you desire.

The problem-centered energy zone resides within thought. There is a separate energy field of solutions that is within the realm of the divine, which is what you can think of as connecting to answers. This is an energy field of clarity where solutions live. This

energy of solutions is a precursor to a lifestyle directly benefited by Divine Guiding Presence. It is true empowerment and one that holistically benefits all. The *energy of solutions* moves beyond karma, good or bad, where you are lifted into pure awareness, and ultimately become divine clarity and light through the physical. This energy field is always available to you, yet not often tapped into because of the incessant focus on fear-based and problem-focused thoughts.

Observe how you are feeling throughout the day and you will get a good idea of the types of thoughts that you are thinking. Often you assume that the way that you are feeling is due to what is happening around you, when often, what is happening is irrelevant, as long as it is not harming you or another. What determines how you are feeling and the reality you believe that you are living is based on the thoughts that you are thinking.

I imagine this *energy of solutions* to be this ever-present swirling vortex of light and pure clarity.

Enveloped within this vortex are divine love, wisdom, and the essence of divine guiding presence. What is most important to understand or have faith in is what this *energy of solutions* can do to powerfully benefit your life daily. The only element that exists in this vortex, or energy, is *the answer*.

The way that this *energy of solutions* works is simple. Every time you focus on the solution to any perceived problem you have, this energy works to clarify, reveal and help you carry out or attain the solution to what is causing you stress, fear, guilt or any other negative emotion you may be feeling in response to the problem that you have defined.

When you are in a habit of reaching for *the energy of solutions*, you are liberated and live in the realm of "love-given," rather than in the energy of problems, which is constricting and in the realm of "love held closely." What it means to live in the realm of "love held closely" is that you are living purely for the self.

In the words of Spirit, "If you hold love to the self, there it stays. If a tree held all its fruit, the fruit would rot, if the fruit given from the tree is not consumed it rots. A tree gives freely its fruit. The fruit is freely consumed. The consumed waters the tree, the tree grows more fruit. Who will water the tree? Who will hold its fruit? What would become of the tree that held its fruit? Now the tree is you, and the fruit is love." When you express openness to accepting and allowing in the *energy of solutions*, you receive back the energy you give out. If you hold tightly onto the desire for a solution without giving anything out to accept a solution, nothing is returned to you and you remain in the energy of problems.

It is in this *energy of solutions* that you align yourself with a clear enlightenment field where you have access to the realm of the divine where answers, do indeed, become clear. Incidentally, the *energy of solutions* is tied directly to the qualities of love—grace, mercy, compassion, etc. It is a pure empowering energy field. When you move into this energy field of solutions, you leave and are in no way connected to the energy of problems. When you say, "there is always a solution" you remind yourself of the fact that you are indeed infinitely guided and supported. Through this declaration, you allow the 99% Element of Divinity to work for you.

As defined in *Love is the Seed: Teachings from the Spirit World*, the 99% Element of Divinity means that for every one step you take in your life, God takes 99 steps for your benefit. So, to take this one step farther, upon declaring, "there is always a solution," you can put to work this 99% Element of Divinity by taking any steps you can to live or be the solution and allow the 99% element to take the rest of the steps and the ultimate solution will be revealed to you.

The beauty of this *energy of solutions* is that you are not required to fully know the solution to your problems. All you are required to do is invite the solution to reveal itself. You begin doing this through the mantra, "There is always a solution."

This statement alone instantly reminds you of the existence of the *energy of solutions* that is always available to you and immediately presents you with a path to two options: (1) surrender your problems or fears to this energy field for resolution or, (2) stay focused on the problem and try to figure out the solution with your mind.

As an example, in response to an event in your life that leaves you thinking thoughts of resentment or anger—often these thoughts will repeat themselves and randomly resurface. What you do is you first take a conscious centering breath and say, "Ok, I know there is always a solution. I am going to relax and accept the light of pure divinity to clearly reveal the answer with grace and ease." And then let it go for the moment and occupy yourself in a way that discourages the cycle of painful thoughts from resurfacing. This does not mean that you are ignoring your emotions or invalidating or undervaluing what you are feeling, it simply means that you consciously align yourself with the solution and allow that declaration to take the weight of that thought off you.

Keep in mind that the *energy of solutions* and this mantra is <u>more powerful</u> than the problems field that thoughts are most often attached to, so by making the solutions declaration through this mantra you have an incredible force working for your benefit.

PRACTICES FOR SUPREME GIFT TWO: THOUGHT

Mantra:

"There is always a solution."

Solutions Declaration:

"Ok, I know there is always a solution. I am going to relax and accept the light of pure divinity to clearly reveal the answer with grace and ease."

"I release this thought with grace and ease."

Request for Help:

"God, my friend, I can't seem to get these thoughts out of my mind. I don't want to feel (NAME FEELINGS) any longer. Instead, I want to feel (NAME FEELINGS). This is how I want to live and be. I surrender this problem to you. I accept the solution to be clearly revealed to me with grace and ease. May I feel your heart in my heart and my heart as a part of your heart. Thank you."

SUPREME GIFT THREE

FREE WILL

"Responsibility is understanding that souls are forged with free will and are responsible for their evolution."

—SUNDAY, NOVEMBER 8, 1981, SESSION 41
LOVE IS THE SEED: TEACHINGS FROM THE SPIRIT WORLD

CHAPTER 5

FREE WILL

"I HAVE THE FREE WILL TO CREATE THE MOST WHOLLY BENEFICIAL OUTCOME."

"I have the free will to create the most wholly beneficial outcome," is one of the most ideal mantras for the supreme gift of *free will*. This mantra compassionately merges with and acknowledges your connection to both the energy of *love* (supreme gift one of love) and the energy of *solutions* (supreme gift two of thought), thus giving you the complete and total empowerment to create and imagine into existence a life that is magnetically charged with wholly beneficial outcomes should you choose, regardless of the karma with which you come into this life to resolve. But more than that, it puts you in charge of your destiny in companionship with the divine guiding presence within you.

This is what you are empowered with upon coming into this life—the full creative power, where you can <u>experience</u> who you really are; you can feel it, demonstrate it and share it. Given that thought creates, free will expresses, and love is the foundation that functions and guides, this free will is the gift that creates <u>tangible</u> results in your life—positive or negative—unique unto you. Without free will, then love and thought would be self-contained and there would be no significant advancement or improvement; there would be little to no creation, little to no benefit to your-*self*, your soul or to others.

> *"Now the soul can follow many paths of development*
> *through intent; and doing by just observing,*
> *the path is longer. The paths that are followed are*
> *recognized by the soul as <u>self</u>-advancement,*
> *<u>soul</u>-advancement, and <u>shared</u>-advancement."*
> —NOTEBOOK #32, PAGE 10,
> *LOVE IS THE SEED: TEACHINGS FROM THE SPIRIT WORLD*

There are two perspectives of free will: (1) the soul's free will to create, which is done through the pure, enlightened energy of love ("love given"), and (2) the personality's free will of thought and action, externally guided, influenced and driven. What is so profound is the supreme trinity alliance of the three supreme gifts: love is the foundation, truth, and wisdom your soul seeks to embody; thought is the "creator"—where you create, imagine and visualize the reality that you want to have; and free will expresses; it is the action and the expression of what you imagine to bring to fruition.

So, when you think of free will from this perspective of coming from a place of love at the seed—that element and supreme truth of God—you conclude that in doing so, you naturally make wholly beneficial conscious decisions.

✻ "(WHOLLY BENEFICIAL) * (CONSCIOUS) * (DECISIONS)"

"Wholly beneficial" meaning that you have greater awareness to and live through the energy of "love-given," in consideration of All.

"Consciousness" meaning that connection to divine love—the very energy of your creation, way of being as soul and the full knowing that <u>all</u> are created equal.

"Decision" meaning the conclusion or resolution, which leads and guides your actions, and making this resolution from the <u>wisest</u>, <u>most divine</u> place.

This is what it means to make "wholly beneficial conscious decisions" through the supreme gift of free will. It is truly magnificent and empowering and can do absolute wonders for your life and of those with whom you come in contact. When you think about your gift of free will to create, free will of thought, free will in action, and so on, you can align your free will choices in a way that benefits both you and the "whole"—all those involved—both here on Earth and in the non-physical spirit world.

I believe that making wholly beneficial conscious decisions is the intended goal of <u>all</u> human creation. It is out of pure love and wisdom that your soul must come to embody through your "free will personality" and essentially live out your free will in this energy of "love-given." This then translates to embodying love's grace, mercy, and compassion, for yourself and others in everything that you do. In essence, it is to think how God "thinks," to work how God works, to give how God gives and to create how God creates.

What this supreme trinity takes is the *personality* part of you to realize the connection to the *soul* part of you. What we know from the book *Love is the Seed: Teachings from the Spirit World* is that the soul projects its free will as a love-given creation and wishes to create all from this energy of love. Through this, your soul projects through your human personality, which is a freely evolving personality that must eventually find itself as a part of your soul.

In the session on Thursday, March 11, 1982, from *Love is the Seed: Teachings from the Spirit World*, a Wise One speaks to this by saying, "The new personality learning and developing with a goal and learning objective can choose on its own, based upon its free will to follow any pursuit that it wishes. Just as a child can choose to run away from its parents, or to try, and do what it pleases without accepting or looking for guidance from guardians or loved ones. The soul is <u>always</u> there within, for any newly experiencing personality."

In other words, personality develops and has its own perception of free will. This perception is influenced mostly by social structures, upbringing, and developed beliefs, so much so that the intention of the soul often gets lost. When this happens, the actions that you take in your life can become misguided because you can only create within the environment you are familiar with. It is only when you can find that connection back to your soul, your true self, that you can guide your free will in accordance with your divine purpose.

For example, if you were raised within an environment where there was a racial divide and you learn certain beliefs toward another race, your free will action can become misguided, leading you to behave violently toward another race or culture. Because of this free will action, let's say, you go to jail where you are surrounded by all races and placed in a cell with someone of a different race than you. As you are forced to live in the same space as this other person, you realize that there are more similarities than differences between the two of you and your beliefs change. And from that day forward, you shift your focus and free will actions from judgment to greater acceptance and understanding, which is more in the energy of love—that energy of your soul. What you have done is reconnected to that divine part of you by your shift from judgment to acceptance.

The Wise One from this session on March 11 continues to say, "The human personality is a being of its own and functions as that being until it, on its own terms, comes to the realization that it is more than a singular adversely alone being." That is to say that the personality part of you must come to the realization that it is a part of a greater soul-self. When you become aware of this greater soul-self, there are almost no limitations to what you can do. The challenge at first becomes that you have an inner voice trying to guide you as well as existing thoughts and beliefs, so there may exist an inner conflict leading you to constantly question what you see and what you hear. That inner voice when followed will lead you to an understanding of your inner being and when you do, you become more of what Spirit terms as an "enlightened soul." If you try to stifle that inner voice by the nature of free will, you can do so.

The benefit to connecting with the free will creative nature of your soul is that you shift your life more consciously for the better in the energy of love-given, which has a domino effect on all others who encounter you, thus benefiting the "whole." Love is an understanding that all are born to choose their destinies, to respect the free will right of others and to accept others' right to give and accept or to deny their destiny.

What more beautiful gift that God has given than to give the creative empowerments to not only benefit your life and soul but also to touch the lives of others. Through this forged free will in pursuit of this service of love, you and all souls living in this human experience choose a path and a role. Here in lies your soul's purpose and endeavor.

Free will as wholly beneficial conscious decisions is where the "personality" part of you makes a conscious connection with your soul, and it is liberating. When you make your free will choices from a wholly beneficial perspective, you change the course of your life and that of others. You do this from a heightened level of consciousness in connection with your soul. This consciousness is connected to love and because you essentially center yourself and think and do in this heightened consciousness in the energy of God— in a wholly beneficial way—you live in a way that you were <u>created</u> to live. It is beautiful when you can touch upon this; you do so by living a solution-centered, loving life making wholly beneficial conscious decisions.

In terms of consciousness, you can say that it exists in this present moment, and yet it is simultaneously connected to your soul—its past and future—because consciousness exists everywhere. The subject of consciousness can be quite foreign. In simple terms, it is the state of being aware. Consciousness is not taught in school, nor is it a subject that often comes up in your daily life. There are a select few people who encourage the practice of connecting to and increasing your level of consciousness, and a select few people who teach how to understand the power of consciousness. Yet through the three supreme gifts you can naturally elevate your level of consciousness to create a life of greater joy here on Earth in form, and it can empower you as soul to evolve exponentially closer to your "wholeness/completeness" with the One Supreme Consciousness, the "I am" of consciousness, of God—of mercy, grace, compassion, and wisdom—of which you are a part.

In other words, when you can be more aware of the empowerment of the energy of love and energy of solutions (through the gift of thought) as it relates to your free will, you put your faith in your higher-self, your higher consciousness, your soul, and that divine guiding presence within you so that you may live out the greater, more fulfilling purpose that you came here to have. You touch upon this awareness when you, as personality, live out your free will in companionship with the divine guidance of love and within the energy of solutions, through thought.

Your consciousness can reach you to the greatest heights when in moments where you are absorbed in pure, silent awareness, fully aware, present and connected. Imagine a time where you felt pure joy and love, as with the birth of your child where you experience the miracle of creation. From conception, growth of each cell, to birth into physical form, you get to directly and personally experience creation from a divine perspective. You get to experience a creation created from this God-energy of "love-given." Every cell gives out of this energy of "love-given" in an ordered process, creating something truly incredible—life. And you are a co-creator in this divine process of life.

And in contrast, a lack of consciousness—a lack of awareness of your thoughts, actions, and your connection to the Divine—can plunge you to the greatest depths. You can find yourself taking paths that are not in alignment with what your soul intended, which does not feel good, and it leads you to question everything about your life. Imagine a time where your thoughts took over, triggering deep emotional pain of which you saw no way out.

❋ The First Free Will Experience

In the book, *Love is the Seed: Teachings from the Spirit World*, Spirit speaks of when souls first began to experiment with free will. They explain how when doing so, souls found that they had the God-given power to create any conditions they thought. As humans formed thoughts, some were erroneous thoughts and created an imbalance in the natural Law of Love.

Such thoughts created new man-made definitions of love. These definitions became structures and humans became more concerned with man-made structures than with the natural Law of Love. These new thoughts were passed down through the ages creating even more new man-made thoughts, definitions, and structures. Today this human experience is so immersed in these new thoughts, definitions, and structures that it leads to war, prejudices, and injustices.

✽ *The Many Paths that Lead to Truth*

The purpose of coming into this life is the pursuit of truth, and what your soul innately knows is that this truth is love. Your personality is not yet aware of this pursuit of love, which leads you to take many paths. Free will is the method by which you choose <u>how</u> you are going to reach that ultimate destination of truth.

In other words, you are creating your own path, or paths, to truth. You will take many paths to truth, some rocky and some smooth. If you make choices that take you down a rocky path, often, according to Spirit, you must travel back that same path to find a smoother path. This is where wholly beneficial conscious decisions and the three supreme gifts become especially powerful because, in this energy, you can, in fact, be lifted from your current rocky path to a smoother path without traveling back over the same one that you had taken.

> *"The paths and highways of experience of life, each excursion is represented by intent . . . Throughout all experience, the soul has the, sometimes, hidden*

> *potential of changing and choosing the paths and roads*
> *to understand truth and God. There are many paths if*
> *the soul wishes to take the bumpy road of hard knocks,*
> *it is but an excursion from the main highway of truth."*
> —TUESDAY, APRIL 18, 1982, SESSION 172,
> *LOVE IS THE SEED: TEACHINGS FROM THE SPIRIT WORLD*

You can imagine in your own life a set of choices you made that led you to many experiences, and to this moment. You have walked a specific path, or set of paths, for a long time. Imagine for a moment that you've been walking on this familiar path. It's smooth and enjoyable *enough* you think—at least enough to "deal" with. Yet, as you go along you find yourself tripping on rocks and pebbles set along the path more and more often. "Stupid rocks," you say, "someone should really clean those up." At some pivotal point, you find yourself at a section where your path divides. You are given a choice—the free will to choose to stay on your familiar path or to take a leap of faith and follow a new path.

This new path can be to change your thoughts and beliefs in a positive way, or it can be to take a new career path or make a change in a relationship. Standing there looking back at the path that you had just been on, you realize that those rocks and pebbles were no coincidence, but divinely placed to get your attention and guide you to take a new path that you were being led to follow all along. A more wholly beneficial path.

While not the most enjoyable or smooth, this path that you had been taking was familiar and predictable. Although feeling unsure of what the new path will be like, in faith, you turn from your old path to begin something brand-new. This new path may start off a bit sloppy because you are, in fact, trying something new, but soon you find this path to be much smoother. This new path that I am referring to is love, which does, in fact, call you to follow it all throughout your life. When you freely and consciously follow this path, the journey to your destination is one of empowerment and companionship.

Let's take, for example, a family counselor who is starting out in a new business as a financial analyst. He works countless hours getting everything that he needs together, goes to networking events, hands out business cards and tries various marketing methods to get business, and while he has some success, it is mostly a struggle. He is doing "all the right things," yet the path to success seems to be consistently rough and challenging. Despite feeling tired and miserable, the more challenging it is to get business, the harder he works.

All throughout this journey, what he does not fully realize is that he is subtly presented in different ways to going back to his first career as a counselor. On occasion, his inner voice would call him to think about making the change back, but he chooses instead to ignore that voice because he still holds a belief that he is only "successful" if he is a prosperous financial analyst.

So, through his free will, he continues taking the path as a financial analyst, ignoring this "calling" back to be a counselor, and he continues to struggle for years. This path of struggle has now become familiar, and despite starting to have a desire to be a counselor again, he is afraid of the unknown. Various questions come up within his mind, "What will people think? Does this mean I am a failure? What if I can't make the money I want?" One day, in a leap of faith, he decides to go back to be a counselor and in a short amount of time, he finds that his life is flowing again, his work is coming easy, he is enjoying those who he counsels and he feels fulfilled as he helps client after client, which is a feeling he never felt as a financial analyst. He was guided to and found the path to love. And through this path to love, he also found financial security and a new belief in what "success" means.

When it comes to expressing your free will, you can take any number of paths in your life in pursuit of purpose, achievement and "something greater." In a session on Saturday, August 21, 1982, Spirit makes an important reference to how to choose your path and what the true meaning is of free will. This reference relates directly to both the personality's perspective and method of expressing free will, and that of the soul's perspective. Spirit sums it up by saying, "When you walk in God's will, you walk in true free will. When you walk in your will, tread wisely for there are many paths within the self."

In other words, if you seek a path solely through the personality aspect of you, which is most often focused through thought and influenced by man-made structures and beliefs, you will take many paths in pursuit of purpose, meaning, achievement and greater joy. Conversely, when you walk in "God's will," you walk along a path that is wholly beneficial, which is true free will. It is free will as it was intended to be—freely expressed from and through the energy of "love-given."

❋ *The Integration of Free Will Creation in Wake State and*
   Dream State

In the book, *Love is the Seed: Teachings from the Spirit World*, Spirit speaks about how you are born into this life through the process of visualization and creation, and it is a "waking dream" in which you are given the free will to create. You are also given symbols—events, people, things—to guide you and provide you answers. And in this waking dream, you experience various realities—from ones that feel good to ones that feel bad. This human experience is temporary, a "waking dream," and through free will—within the energy of both love and through the gift of thought—you have all that is needed to create the dream of our choosing.

In Notebook #33, Page 1 included in the book *Love is the Seed: Teachings from the Spirit World*, Spirit refers to the "wake state" that is your daily life and how in both this wake state and in the "sleep state" the personality and soul access free will to create. It is in the sleep state that the soul contacts the Greater Self and other internal beings, as well as random thoughts. This sleep state is a reality in and of itself and reflects your wake state. In both the wake state and the sleep state, there is imagination, visualization, and creation at work.

The personality during waking hours through free will visualizes, imagines and acts out thoughts and they become reality. In both the sleep state and in the wake state, you are creating and living out a reality unique to you. Perhaps on occasion in your sleep state, you have experienced being aware that you are dreaming and with this awareness, you are able to create any reality that you wish. I recall this happening on a few occasions where I became aware that I was in a dream and knew that I could control what I wanted to happen in the dream. In the dream, I became aware of this free will to create. These experiences are enlightening because you realize that there is little difference between your free will abilities in wake state and in a sleep state. You are, in essence, living out the "waking dream" of life.

❋ When You Have Wise-Eyes
The wisdom of this perspective of free will done from the energy of love and through thought from the *energy of solutions* is referenced in the book *Love is the Seed: Teachings from the Spirit World* when a Wise One talked about how what is created from the heart—from this energy of love-given and from the honest integrity from within—that you receive back the same multiplied many times; and that love reverberates and grows when given freely. Upon understanding this, you can have what the spirit world terms as "wise eyes." Keep in mind that you can have wise eyes and still error and go down a path that is not the most beneficial, but you get back on a more beneficial path more quickly and you are able to stay on the path more consistently.

> *"It is better to pursue an error than to sit and stagnate,*
> *for there is no growth and no understanding."*
> —WISE GUIDE, MONDAY, FEBRUARY 1, 1982, SESSION 106,
> *LOVE IS THE SEED: TEACHINGS FROM THE SPIRIT WORLD*

❋ *How Wholly-Beneficial Free Will Affects Karma*

In the book, *Love is the Seed: Teachings from the Spirit World*, Spirit talks often about how before deciding to incarnate into form, a soul goes through a process of "study" where the soul reviews past life experiences and seeks to heal unresolved experiences and "emotional baggage." For example, this study can include looking at aspects of emotions such as unworthiness and focus your experience at this vibrational level of unworthiness to learn the truth of love that inherent within you.

There is a fascinating correlation between free will and your soul's plan upon deciding to incarnate into this life. Given that most souls come into this human existence to resolve a debt—negative karma—from which to learn the truth of love, it is, in fact, possible to resolve a debt without fully experiencing the suffering of the negative karma. You can do this through free will when that free will is made from the perspective of that which is wholly beneficial.

Let's say for example, before your birth, your soul planned to experience a set of circumstances within the energy of greed that led to you losing your professional reputation. Yet upon coming into this free will forged life—given to each with whom you come in contact—you become enlightened to the healing energy of generosity and kindness. Upon becoming enlightened, through your free will choice, you decide to change your actions from greed to generosity and in doing so, you end up not losing your professional reputation. You found your way to a more wholly beneficial path, out of the energy of greed, so the experience of losing your reputation is no longer needed.

Another example is if in a past life you held the false belief that you were unworthy of being loved, and it led you to a great fear of being alone, so much so that you became an emotional abuser to a loved one. Upon review in your afterlife, you desired to balance out the experience by reincarnating into a life where you planned to be abused in various relationships.

In doing so, you also chose to carry these feelings of unworthiness and fear of being alone, for healing this emotional baggage. This karmic debt of being abused is not to punish your lifetime as an abuser, but to experience the opposite perspective with the same types of emotions, so that you may heal and further learn the supreme truth of love. Free will comes into play at any moment within your life. In this example, you may be awakened by a person who showed kindness, helping you realize your worth, and as a result, you make a conscious choice to terminate your relationship with your current abuser. This choice then leads you to seek out experiences that reinforce your feeling and knowing of your worthiness and you ultimately end the cycle of the repetitive abusive relationships your soul intended you to experience before incarnation. This karmic debt is fully released because the underlying feelings of unworthiness are healed.

❋ *Being Born Again the Moment You Know What You Want*
When you find that circumstances in your life are not what you wish them to be and they are causing you to experience suffering or other negative emotions such as anger, resentment, et al., you may feel that there is no one to help you. So, when you acknowledge that

aspects of your life are not what we wish them to be, you innately know "something needs to change." You may question God and wonder why God is not making things better, why God is allowing such things to happen to you, and why God is not helping you. Yet, as expressed by a Wise One in the book *Love is the Seed: Teachings from the Spirit World*, God <u>has</u> helped you; God has given you the greatest gift out of love, which is your free will, as well as God's constant companionship.

In the words of a Wise One in Notebook #17, Page 5, "That forged free will that for all is freedom, no matter where you and what your circumstances are. Slave or king, healthy or sick; within you lies your future, past and present to guide, change and direct, for there are many ways for one to be reborn. You will have many lives and experiences here on Earth, but one can be reborn the moment the choice is made and pursued." What this says is that you, and all, can be "reborn" the moment the choice is made and free will is pursued.

Some are born into this life already knowing that they want to be happy and they seek out ways of being happy, despite challenges and setbacks. And some are born not knowing what they really want, and they allow their external environment to guide them, which often, does not work for their benefit and they never find their way. And then there are those who find themselves on a path of challenges, yet they get enlightened in one way or another to the infinite love of God and they learn to love themselves and give more to others and they are essentially "born again;"—this time living more and more each day from a perspective of love and in the energy of solutions. It is a work in progress and there are setbacks, but over time your life completely changes for the better. This can be at <u>any</u> point in your life.

❋ *God as Your Greatest Friend*

When you make wholly beneficial consciousness decisions, you also make divine agreements that can be made deep within the subconscious with those in the spirit world, with other souls, for love and that benefits all. This can be done directly through prayer or meditation. If prayer or meditation is something that does not appeal to you right now, you can simply have a conversation with God, with the faith and knowing that you will always be met with compassion, grace, mercy, and love. You can say, "God, my friend, I want to do what is going to be best for me and everyone involved. Please make the path to action clear to me." Believe that God is your greatest friend because God, indeed, is. In the words of Spirit, "God's purpose is to empower us through love. What we do with that is our free will choice."

It was in a Wednesday, October 20, 1982 session that a Wise One said, "Then God desired companionship and created equally all and each to be with God, creating with God, forever loving. Each creation knew the principles, knew what they were, and yet only through giving could they come to understand that they were within all and yet themselves. Each will be with God in truth and that decision is made when it is realized that it is not meant to be alone." You are a love of God and always a part of God.

❀ *When What You Seek to Accomplish Seems Just Out of Reach*

When you act from a place of love and you are reaching higher to attain all that you feel drawn to achieve through this God-gifted free will that you are forged with, you may find that what you wish to acquire is just out of reach. In this instance, I want you to imagine that as you are reaching high to acquire what you desire, there is a loving force helping to lift you up. This is God at work to help you achieve that which you desire. It is much like when a small child desires to acquire an object just out of reach. They are reaching and stretching as far as their abilities allow them. Knowing they are trying their best, you come and gently lift them just enough, so they get the object and find success. This is what it is like when God is at work for you. You reach as high as you can and God lifts you the rest of the way—God is that divine guiding force at work.

❀ *You are the Instrument of Beautiful Creation*

When you hold a pen in your hand to write a beautiful poem, you use the pen as an instrument by which to express a creation—to make the creation tangible. You do so by your free will to create and you imagine something beautiful and something that feels good. As you begin to write, ease and flow begin to carry through the pen and it is as if the pen is writing this creation and you are simply helping to guide the pen. Now imagine that you are that pen, and God is that guiding force.

You are like a pen in the hand of God. <u>You</u> are the instrument. This is what love-given free will is—this divine guiding, gentle force, or energy guiding your creation and allowing the pen, you, to take over and create. Ask yourself what it is that you wish to create—"what is it that I really want?"—and then know that you are cradled in the hand of God to help guide your creation.

You are only required to pursue or create in the direction of that which you want, and that which you want will find its way to and through you. Believe in this guiding force as your support, your best friend, and have faith in that, and when you do, you set yourself up for truly beautiful things in your life here, now and forevermore. God is with you and you are with God.

> "Free will allows for all, for without free will then would not souls be merely puppets to dance to the tune of their creator and never in themselves create love or think? For without free will they could never have the original desire to express, for their thought would come from a creator and not from themselves. So, all beings and created beings must have free will."
> —Monday, March 15, 1982, Session 137,
> *Love is the Seed: Teachings from the Spirit World*

PRACTICES FOR SUPREME GIFT THREE:
FREE WILL

MANTRA:
"I have the free will to create the most wholly beneficial outcome."

QUESTION:
"What is it that I <u>really</u> want?"

DECLARATION AND REQUEST FOR HELP:
"God, my friend, I want to do what is going to be best for me and everyone involved. Please make the path to action clear to me."

CHAPTER 6

THE HARMONIOUS INTEGRATION OF THE THREE SUPREME GIFTS

Here we have come to the end of this book, which ironically turns out to be, what I hope is the beginning of a more wholly beneficial, joyful and healing life for you with a greater awareness of and the knowledge to utilize the three supreme gifts that you are forged with upon coming into this life. These three supreme gifts are the very foundation by which you now have harmoniously connected that <u>spiritual</u> part of you with the <u>physical</u> part of you.

Within these pages, it has been my hope that with a better understanding of these three gifts that you know, without a doubt, that you have all you need to transform your life here and now, move beyond negative karmic and thought patterns not benefiting you, and ultimately change the course of your life in a more wholly beneficial way. With this, you are guided to a deeper understanding of the depth of each element of love, thought, and free will. The mantras provided are meant to directly benefit your life, on a practical day-to-day basis, affecting every aspect of your life.

With a better understanding of your connection to God—that divine guiding presence within <u>you</u>—and your soul's connection to your physical, conditioned existence as personality, you can strengthen and enhance your ability to get the absolute most enjoyment from your life. And in doing so, you can more fully live out your purposes with less stress and greater fulfillment; that now, through a better understanding of these gifts, my hope is that you find that your role and responsibilities as mother, father, spouse, employee, and so on become more divinely directed, and the way that you view and respond to your life and your role in it is one that is more holistically beneficial, where you can be of service to yourself and to others.

This practical, divinely guided approach to self-mastery through these gifts is intended to be a guide by which you consciously choose how you want to live your life and what you want to create. It is the <u>integration</u> of these gifts that lead you to the living of life in an energy of blessings begets blessings. Integration happens when individual, specialized parts unite to create something of greater value and benefit.

❋ The Integration

Each of the three supreme gifts is uniquely specialized in and of itself. Each has their own system in which they function as a part of a larger system of your life. In the case of your soul and personality, they are a specialized part of your evolution. In a Monday, February 1, 1982 session referenced in the book *Love is the Seed: Teachings from the Spirit World*, Spirit references this system by saying, "Truth operates upon the laws of thought, love and free will. <u>All actions</u> are because of and in response to thought, love and free will. Each system of reality no matter when focused, exhibits a reaction to this truth. On Earth, with the system or order of the human being, there exist many man-made structures, concepts, beliefs, governments, societies, individuals, theories, and all exhibit and function within truth, love, free will and thought." To state more clearly, all creation works within a system. Love is a system made up of a combination of parts, or elements or qualities, forming the unitary whole by which the gift of love in its entirety works. The same holds true for thought and free will. And when each system functions and is used as it was intended, what you get is a harmonious union of empowerments.

And when these three gifts are integrated, meaning that when each gift in their "wholeness," or system, are connected, they move your life toward a harmonious flow from the inside out. They allow you the full empowerment to create. When integrated, you, as the personality experiencing this life, become more flexible to change, inspired toward actions that come with greater flow, and you more often feel the excitement that comes from engaging in new ways to your life.

Let's reflect on each of these gifts as their own specialized system: <u>Love</u> is a specialized "whole," in part, comprising of what was focused on in the chapter for the supreme gift of love—compassion, grace, mercy, and patience. <u>Thought</u> is a specialized "whole" comprising of, 1) the power of your analytical mind and 2) the empowerment that comes from thoughts that are in the *energy of solutions*. <u>Free will</u> is a specialized "whole" comprising of liberty of thoughts and actions, that when born from a wholly beneficial perspective can benefit all aspects of your life, including your relationship to yourself and <u>all</u> others.

When these specialized "wholes" from each of the three supreme gifts are <u>integrated</u>, you have all that you need to attain self-mastery and transform your life.

❈ *The Self-Mastery Formula*

When you add the three supreme gifts together, they form the full creative empowerment over your life.

(1) Understanding how love is demonstrated in this life (divine love and how it translates in your life) and taking action from the energy of *love-given* (mantra: "compassion, grace, mercy, patience.")

(2) (PLUS+) observing, training and guiding your thoughts in a way that manifests positive emotions and feelings (which live in the body and carry a life of their own—from lifetime to lifetime) (mantra: "There is always a solution.")

(3) (PLUS+) understanding how to best utilize your free will (mantra: "I have the free will to create the most wholly beneficial outcome.")

(4) (EQUALS=) the <u>full</u> creative empowerment over your life in alignment with and in the energy of divine guiding presence—that existence of God that is within you.

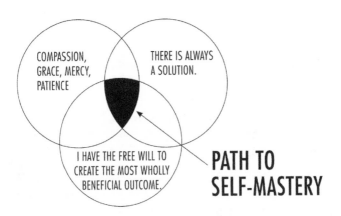

PATH TO
SELF-MASTERY

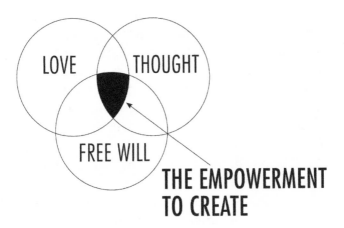

THE EMPOWERMENT
TO CREATE

"What matters is not that one accepts certain theories or rejects them, it is that one comes to an internal understanding and creates and lives and exists and functions as God intends."
—WEDNESDAY, JULY 7, 1982, SESSION 201,
LOVE IS THE SEED: TEACHINGS FROM THE SPIRIT WORLD

❊

Integration of the Mantras
"Through compassion, grace, mercy, and patience
there is always a solution
by which I can create wholly beneficial outcomes
here, now, forevermore."

❊ Mantras in Practice

The mantras included with each gift are meant to help you refocus yourself. First, they are meant to make you feel better in any given moment and second, to naturally bring you into an energy that reflects your true nature, ultimately leading you to self-mastery in a way that allows you to fully enjoy and be fully present in your life. You can enjoy greater clarity and peace in your life.

What makes the mantras in this book so powerful is that they work in complete harmony with one another. For example, when you cycle through the two mantras for thought and free will, with the mantra for love being at the foundation, you are fully and divinely empowered in <u>any</u> situation. And, when it comes to free will and making free will decisions and taking free will actions, you will continually go back to the mantras for love and thought.

In the journey of your life, you might be sparked to begin to make some sort of change from any one of the three supreme gifts. Your life's circumstance might first spark love and from there you work through the gift of thought and then free will. In another circumstance, your life circumstances might first spark thoughts and feelings that you wish to be different and from there, you go through the process of first connecting with the energy of solutions through the gift of thought, then that of love and then proceed with expressing through free will. And lastly, your life circumstances might first spark a desire to immediately want to act and make a change. So, you work through the supreme gift of your free will, then work through the supreme gift of thought, while simultaneously ensuring that every step and action along the way reflects the energy and gift of love. I will share three stories that illustrate this now.

CIRCUMSTANCE SPARKED BY LOVE

"compassion, grace, mercy, patience"
In the following circumstance sparked by love, let's imagine for a moment that you are a young girl who finds herself pregnant and alone at 17 years old. You realize that you are in no position to raise a child now in your life and be able to provide for him appropriately without limitation. What is sparked within you is a deep love for this child, which translates to compassion, grace, mercy, and patience. Compassion, grace, and mercy for this little life growing within you and patience that you must embody knowing that despite not being ready to care for this child now, that one day you will be able to fully provide for your child. You must now work through your thoughts.

Through the gift of thought, you reassure yourself that everything will be ok by reciting the mantra, "there is always a solution." Several scenarios race through your mind on what you should do. You know that you want to carry your baby to term, but you waver on whether to keep your son and do your best to raise him knowing that it will be a struggle and stress on you both, or if it will be best to give your son up for adoption. It is your free will to choose. There is a deep internal conflict because you do, in fact, love your baby.

In the energy of love, you decide that the most wholly beneficial course of action is to lovingly allow your son to be adopted. With this wholly beneficial, loving decision made, you research and interview various couples in your determination to find the very best set of parents to which to give your beloved son. What this example illustrates is a deep love for all involved and deciding based on that love. You have lovingly given your son better opportunities in his life that you could not yet provide, allowed those unable to have children to be his parents and you also showed love and compassion for yourself by finishing high school and making plans to go to college and pursue a career, thus setting you up to raise a family in the future.

CIRCUMSTANCE SPARKED BY THOUGHT

"There is always a solution."
In the following circumstance sparked by thought, let's take as an example that you have an argument with your sister that leads to the two of you no longer speaking to one another. During your disagreement, various thoughts go through your mind—"I can't believe she said that to me," "she is so self-centered," "after all that I have done for her and this is how she treats me," "she has never supported the things that

I am excited about," and the list goes on, one thought leading to the next. These thoughts bring up feelings of anger, blame, disappointment and sadness. Recalling the mantra from thought, you know that there is *always a solution.* With this, you also know that you can only do what is in your control and you can't control another.

From this energy of solutions from the gift of thought, you integrate in aspects of the gift of love by acknowledging in a compassionate and merciful way her perspective. You have compassion as you recognize that she too is suffering and despite feeling angry yourself, you wish to help alleviate her suffering. You are merciful as you do your very best to forgive her for what she said or did. As you embrace mercy, you begin the process of releasing resentment.

As you work through the gift of love, you then come to a point that you need to act. It is your free will choice in what your next step will be, and what you will do and say to your sister. You decide that the most wholly beneficial outcome will be to write your sister a compassionate letter acknowledging the good in her, expressing the reason behind how you are feeling and proposing what you are willing and able to do to heal the relationship. You then decide to allow her to decide, without any judgment or assumptions on your part, whether she too wants to make efforts to mend the relationship. What this example illustrates is how thought sparked a desire for change and the process of then focusing from a loving perspective and coming up with a wholly beneficial solution, by honoring yourself, your sister and your relationship.

CIRCUMSTANCE SPARKED BY FREE WILL

"I have the free will to create the most wholly beneficial outcome."

In the following circumstance sparked by free will, let's take as an example that you are in a job that no longer fulfills you. You innately know that something needs to change. You have the free will to stay and have a guaranteed paycheck, or you have the free will to leave your job without knowing yet what that will mean for you and your family financially. From the perspective of the supreme gift of free will you know that you have the free will to create the most wholly beneficial outcome.

What you do then from this perspective is you use the supreme gift of thought to determine a set of possible solutions in relation to the financial impact of leaving your job as well as the workload burden your absence might impose on those with whom you work. Simultaneously to this, you are lovingly taking into consideration all those who will be impacted by your decision. What you decide to do is you set a goal timeline of how long you are willing to stay at your job until you find a new job, ensuring that while you are at your current job you get everything organized and as much taken care of as possible, to make the transition easier for everyone, when you do find that next job opportunity and decide to leave.

❀ What is Sparked When a Loved One Dies

In the book *Love is the Seed: Teachings from the Spirit World*, there is an entire chapter on "Death." This is an especially important topic to explore as it relates to the three supreme gifts because when you are deep in sorrow and heartbreak, nothing seems to feel good, taste good, sound good, or look good. You feel that your whole world is turned upside-down. You feel that you are so deeply lost that you can't see how you will find your way out of what you are experiencing. Simply reaching for better feeling thoughts even seems out of reach. When you feel so lost and out of touch with your own life, this is where repeating words, a mantra, can begin to pull you out. This is a divine truth and the very essence and purpose of the three supreme truths.

As you repeat the mantras more often, you begin to rekindle your belief in the truth of the words. It begins to feel like your soul is consoling you, supporting you, speaking to you and healing you. And this is what is happening. It is then that you start to have brief moments where you feel just a little better, a little more alive and a little more "human," where you can start to function again. As you continue the mantras, these moments become less and less brief and you begin to feel better more often. These mantras allow you to pull yourself out of the thoughts causing continued suffering and they guide you to expand on the love that you shared with that someone who died. Eventually, this love expands and helps to fill in the void that is left from their death. Repeating the mantras can help you heal. "(Today I give myself) compassion, grace, mercy, and patience," "there is always a solution (to how I am feeling)," and "I have the free will to create the most wholly beneficial outcome (from this day forward)."

What these examples illustrate is that although the worldly way still goes on, circumstances and events continue, you have the most empowering gifts to enjoy the moments and days of your life. And the divine energy within you has shifted in a way where you no longer identify with and get continually sucked into the negative emotional effects of the outside circumstances of your life. When you live from a place where you embody love, harness your thoughts in a way that they are of service to you, and guide your free will in a wholly beneficial way, eventually you become the <u>very essence</u> of that which you practice and you allow the divine guiding presence to manifest all the good that you wish to create for this life and beyond.

So, imagine and picture, study and learn, take on more positive thoughts, emotions and attitude, nurture your body well with nutrition and exercise, live in a solutions mindset, acknowledge divine aspects within you, and relax in the knowing that God is always with you.

When you shift your life from perceived problem after problem, to enjoying a flow where you feel liberated with clarity and a greater connection to the universal energy of God of which you are a part, you see <u>all</u> life in a different way. When you live out of love and compassion for another, you see God is available to you and through you, that you are no more or no less than any other human on the Earth; you see that life is infinite and love is the way of all. You see another as "shoes you once walked in."

This shift does not mean that you are or need to be completely self-*less,* but soul-*full,* where you are able and willing to openly give of yourself in a loving and merciful way. And in a way, that honors yourself and others' free will. You put yourself in a position to be that wholly beneficial essence for others. The art of self-love is the act of self-compassion and when you treat and care for yourself where you can be more whole and complete, you are exponentially more of value to others. It begins with believing <u>you are enough</u>. It is as simple, and sometimes as difficult, as that.

My hope that through the mantras that you now naturally align yourself with the healing enlightened energy of divine love, giving you a smoother path to the blessed, beneficial life, you are meant to have. It is the God-given empowerment forged upon you to make the best of where you are right now and transform your future starting this very moment.

As you have this human experience—living through the *personality* part of you—and embody the three supreme gifts, you can find the inner peace and healing that you seek for yourself and desire to share with others. You begin to see how you can touch people with who <u>you</u> are, and you can leverage what knowledge and talents that you have gained in this life, in companionship with your soul, your Higher Self and in companionship with God. <u>This</u> is what you can do, every day—<u>choose</u> how you want to live.

Having worked in branding for many years with professionals from various backgrounds, I regularly talk with those who have a deep desire to be of service to others through their work. And through an authentic branding process, they realize that they each have something unique to give to others or a unique way in which they offer their services to make their clients' lives just a little easier and more enjoyable. Each professional with whom I have worked comes from a place of love—a love for others, a love for giving and a love for creating. What manifests through this is often a restructuring of thoughts and beliefs in the true value of what they provide for others and ultimately a list of ways in which any action that they take in their business is one that is beneficial for them as they reach for higher levels of success and beneficial for those with which they work. Through this, they help to create their own destiny or path to truth, through their free will personality, while benefiting the "whole"—all those with whom they come in contact.

"The justice that each possess is the love of God that through forged free will all will individually and collectively create their destiny and path to the truth. The truth is that love is the seed of all creation, of all being, of all."
—NOTEBOOK #23, PAGE 15,
LOVE IS THE SEED: TEACHINGS FROM THE SPIRIT WORLD

❋ *Faith in What the Eyes Can't See but the Heart Can Feel*
While is it not easy to find your way through your challenges and suffering, when you have faith in what you can't see, you can count on your heart to feel and eventually you will be met with "truth." I love this story about my great-grandmother Julia. She was a wise, faithful and feisty woman who prayed every single afternoon. She was praying one day when a man came into her house and tried to take her

jewelry, even the rings that she was wearing, and she fought him off. Years after her passing, in one of the sessions with Spirit that my father channeled in the early 1980s, my great-grandmother came through and she said something that is truly beautiful and eye-opening. She said, "little did I know that all those times that I was praying to Jesus, that he was sitting right beside me the whole time."

Practicing and living in a way where you continually strive to implement these three supreme gifts does not mean that you never do wrong, or feel anger or judgment; it means that you are willing to, alongside God—and from the divine within you—try your best to embody the light of love, grace, mercy, and the giver of empowerments. This can translate in giving of your time, attention or money, speaking with greater compassion and being more accepting of others and of yourself within the circumstances in your life. It is trying your best to not see yourself as a victim of your circumstances. but as a participant within the circumstance. It is with creative and free will empowerments that you can shift any area of your life to one that works best for you. It is to look at others not as your enemy, but as another soul on their own journey of experiencing who <u>they</u> really are. So, it is through a better knowing of these three supreme gifts that you can benefit your own life, as well as help others to experience and see that for themselves, the magnificence of who they are.

The true beauty about this aspect of being a part of God is that at any moment, you can <u>choose</u> a <u>path of empowerment</u> when you relax in the knowing that what you <u>already</u> have is all that you need to create the life of your choosing. What you have are love, thought, and free will.

> *"One final statement. Do what is in your heart always. Ask for guidance and you shall receive it. And then do what you do without guilt or sorrow."*
> —SATURDAY, OCTOBER 23, 1982, SESSION 253,
> *LOVE IS THE SEED: TEACHINGS FROM THE SPIRIT WORLD*

ABOUT THE AUTHOR

LISA HROMADA is a speaker of timeless spiritual teachings inspired by divine experiences documented in her first book, *Love is the Seed: Teachings from the Spirit World*. She shares a simple, yet profound message: You have all that you need to create the life of your choosing. Lisa brings a practical approach to understanding the truth of love and the creation of Soul, and how to implement spiritual teachings in your life to create greater joy. She engages audiences with personal stories of connections with the spirit world and she explores core teachings outlined in her books.

Website: https://www.LoveIsTheSeed.com

CPSIA information can be obtained
at www.ICGtesting.com
Printed in the USA
LVHW092057180819
627847LV00006B/35/P

9 781620 062012